The Best of

PRIVATE EYE

ONE

or

The Anatomy of Neasden

EX LIBRIS

Mavis Tharg

NEASDEN CITY LIBRARY

Tesco Road, Neasden Parade. Neasden, N.W.10

This book should be returned to the library from which it was borrowed on or before the last date marked below. Unless it is renewed, a charge of 1d. is made for each day or part of a day it is retained after the date due.

-1. APR. 1970

[illegible]

-4. MAY 1970

[illegible]

-5. JUN 1970

24 JUN 1970

16—EVENING ARGUS, Saturday, May 6, 1972

Trains back to normal

By GORDON GREIG

FIVE Ministers were sacked by Mr Heath yesterday in a hard new attack on unemployment.

Daily Mail

MAYOR LOOKS OVER NEW MODEL

The Londoner

Doctor in sex case loses his appeal

Yorkshire Post

Sewage plant on sea front might smell, expert says

The Times

Plagues of Venus

FROM A CORRESPONDENT IN SAN FRANCISCO

The Department of Health, Education and Welfare estimates that 2.5m Americans, more than 10 per cent of the population, will develop gonorrhoea this year—it is now the most commonly reported infectious disease in the United States—and that 100,000 will catch syphilis, now the fourth most common disease. This epidemic has burst upon Americans after a period when it seemed that venereal disease was declining under the impact of antibiotics. It appears to coincide with increased use of the birth control pill and most of its victims are young.

"Clearly new tools are needed," said Dr Bruce Webster, president of the American Social Health Association and the head of the National Commission on Venereal Disease which submitted its report to HEW last week.

Economist

Bodies in the garden are a plant says wife

PORT OF SPAIN, Trinidad,

Hong Kong Standard

Mr. Vallois, hotel worker

● In yesterday evening's report on the St. Peter runway protest meeting, Mr. P. P. Vallois, of St. Peter, was inadvertently quoted as saying that he wanted to say a few words as "a dirty old worker". In fact it should have read "as an hotel worker".

Jersey Evening Post

Dublin has grave cemetery problem

The Evening Press, Dublin

Big cuts to be made at hospital

Manchester Evening News

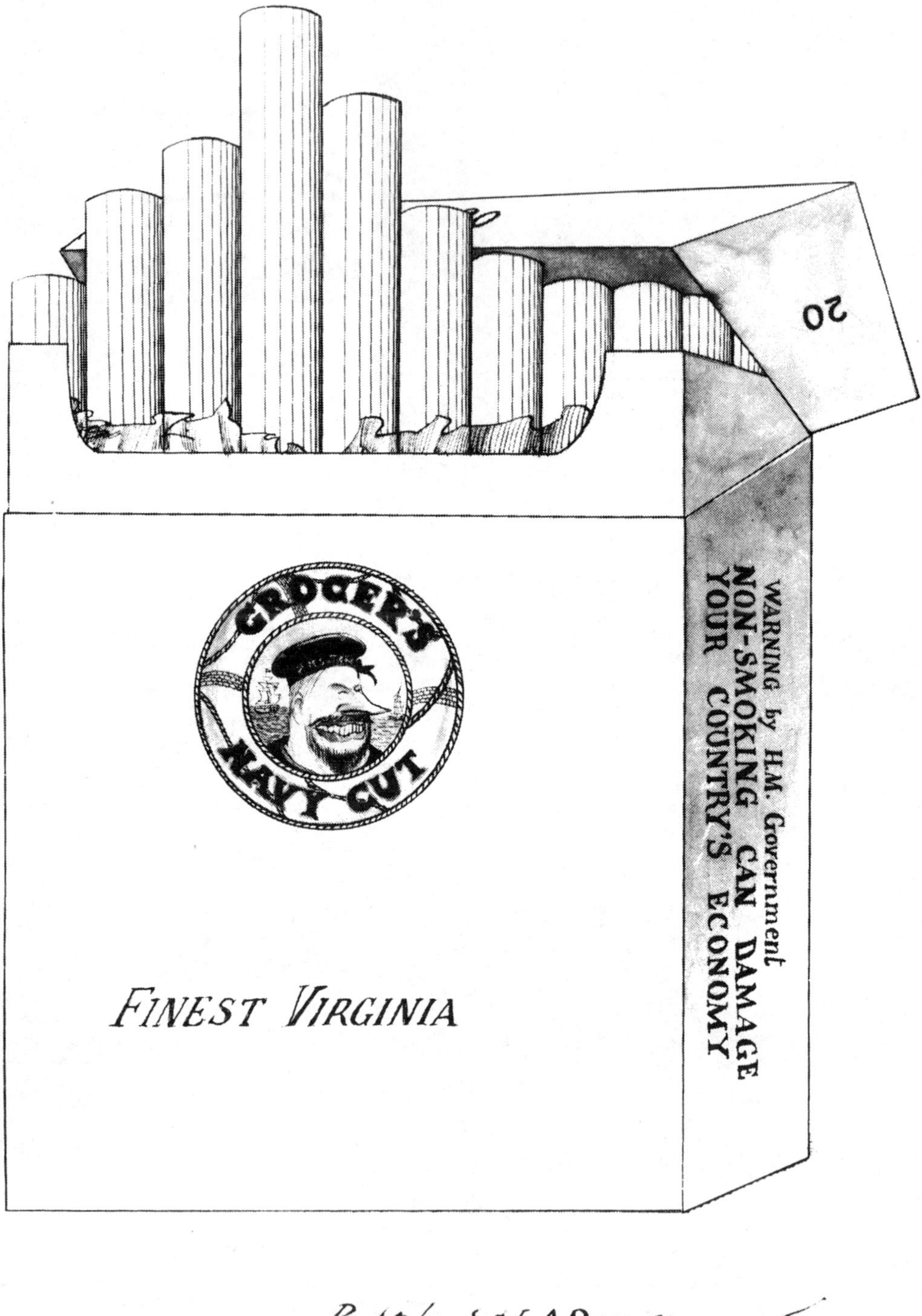
20
GROCER'S
NAVY CUT
FINEST VIRGINIA
WARNING by H.M. Government
NON-SMOKING CAN DAMAGE
YOUR COUNTRY'S ECONOMY
Ralph STEADman

The Best of PRIVATE EYE ONE

or

The Anatomy of Neasden

QUARTET BOOKS · LONDON

Published by Quartet Books Limited 1973
27 Goodge Street, London W1P 1FD

First published in Great Britain by Private Eye Productions Ltd
in association with Andre Deutsch Ltd as *The Best of Private Eye 1972*

ISBN 0 704 31056 2

Printed in Great Britain by Anchor Press Ltd, Tiptree, Essex.

This book is published in a limited edition of 800 million copies, each one printed on hand-woven Neasdilon and bound in buckram-style cardboard

This is No....46,872.........

INTRODUCTION

by LORD GNOME

I have been asked by the publishers to provide an introduction to this book. However, as they are not prepared to offer any money for this arduous task, I have felt it only right to decline their offer.

E. Strobes,
pp. Lord Gnome,
Villa Disraeli,
Cap Gris Nez,
France/Sud

PRIVATE EYE MAGAZINE

PRIVATE EYE IS PROUD TO ANNOUNCE NEXT WEEK THE START OF THE MOST ASTONISHING NEWSPAPER SERIES IN THE HISTORY OF THE WORLD

THE NEASDEN HISTORY OF BRITAIN

In 2789 parts, complete with gold-style binderettes in hand-tooled Gnomitex, wall-to-wall visual aids, working models, long-playing gramophone records featuring the voices of some of the greatest names in history, suits of armour of the type worn at the battle of Muswell Hill and facsimiles of such famous documents as the Doomday Book, Magna Charter and the first edition of the Observer Colour Supplement.

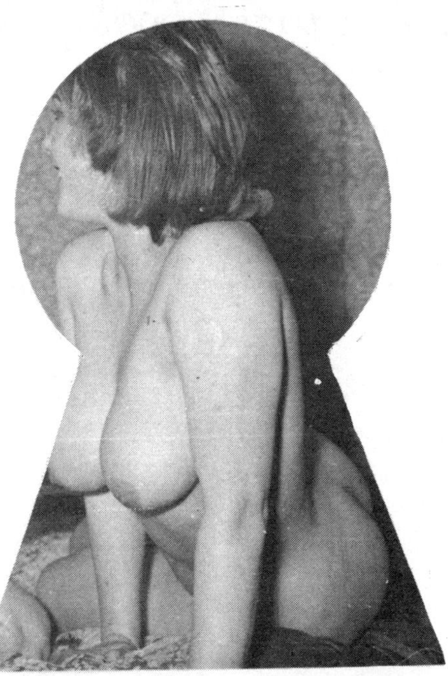

WHAT DID QUEEN BOADICEA LOOK LIKE IN BED?

World-famous artists and photographers combine to bring alive the past as you never would have thought it possible!

PERSPECTIVE

DAILY Mirror PHEW WHAT A SCORCHER!

HOW THE GREAT FIRE OF LONDON OF 1886 MIGHT LOOK IN THE GET-UP-AND-GO LANGUAGE OF TODAY!

This graphic reconstruction draws on such contemporary records as Dr Samuel Johnson's famous "Diary" and the entry under "Great Fire Of London" in the Encyclopaedia Britannica.

BRITAIN'S HERITAGE – TODAY'S TALKING POINT

FOR THE PAST 15 WEEKS, A TEAM OF HAND-PICKED SCHOLARS FROM WORLD-FAMOUS NEASDEN UNIVERSITY HAS BEEN WORKING ROUND-THE-CLOCK TO BRING YOU THE WHOLE RICH TAPESTRY OF BRITAIN'S HERITAGE AS IT HAS NEVER BEEN BROUGHT TO YOU BEFORE.

WHERE DID THE BRITISH COME FROM?

Millions of years before the Romans came, Britain could have been inhabited by men such as the one above. He is Lunchtime O'Booze, the world-famous writer, directly descended from the O'Boicheoiaths, a terrible nomadic tribe, known by their red-faces and habit of lying around all day quaffing mead from the horns of oxen.

A VERY BAD PAINTING OF THE TYPE which the Colour Supplements are currently printing in a desperate attempt to get on the historical bandwagon (as seen on TV).

DISCOVERY

WHAT IS THE SECRET OF STONEHENGE?

The Neasden Engineering Faculty has calculated that it would take 4000 men 11 years to drag the thousand-ton monographs from the nearest railway station at Salisbury to within easy walking distance of the A 3191. How many men would have to order the Neasden History of Britain before Lord Gnome could show a profit of £2,301,429 on his original investment of £1,500 ?

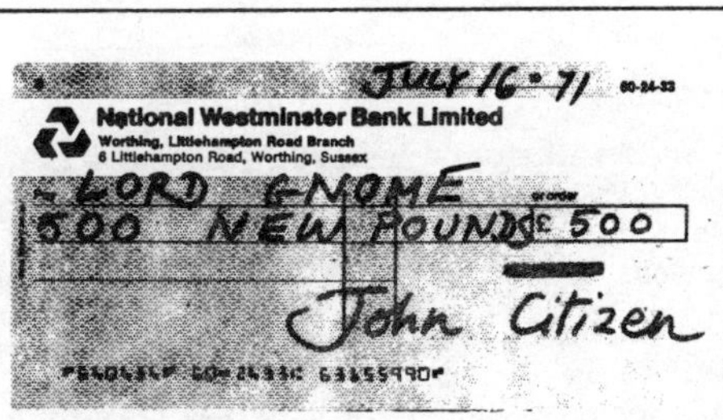

An authentic lifelike facsimile of the type of cheque which it is hoped millions of Britons will be signing in the next few minutes as they order THE NEASDEN HISTORY OF BRITAIN - the unique passport to historical knowledge.

THE GODFREY WINSOME INTERVIEW

Little Boy Lost

It seems like only yesterday that he was on our TV screens almost every hour of the day with his pudding basin haircut and infectious schoolboy grin.

And yet today Desmond Nit is a regular visitor to the Neasden Labour Exchange (or Social Security Centre as it is now politely called) where he draws his weekly pittance of £69.

Oh Dear

Desmond shot to stardom 14 years ago as the first ever mental defective to compere a radio programme. His half-witted "patter" immediately aroused the sympathy of the public and before he knew where he was he had become a star.

Soon he had graduated to TV and *The Desmond Nit Show* in which he interviewed fellow defectives about their lives.

Horror

But then suddenly the bright lights faded. The fickle public moved on to someone new and Desmond was left out in the cold without so much as a by your leave.

Today, despite his terrible setbacks, he is as bright and cheerful as ever. I took the Number 9 bus to Baverstock Hill in Neasden where Desmond lives in a tiny terraced house with his wife Beryl. It was a far cry from the days of wine and roses when he held court in the Maharajah Suite of the David Frost Hotel, Mayfair.

Tear Stained

I asked him if he wanted to go back to his old job on TV. "Course I do, you daft old bugger" he snarled with the familiar charm. "You don't get to be a fantastic star like I was if you're a complete bloody moron."

With a flash of his old boyish enthusiasm, he expectorated violently in my face. I asked him if he had any regrets.

"All I ask is £1000 a week," he snapped. "I mean it's not going to break the Bank of England is it ? A bloke like me is worth ten times that amount."

His wife Beryl came in bringing with her a welcome tea-tray piled high with piping hot muffins, scrumptious buttered toast spread thickly with oozing golden honey, delicious brandy snaps filled with rich , thick Devonshire cream, giant sized gateaux and lemon meringue pies overflowing with juicy hot chocolate sauce.

Disgusting

"I suppose you're one of those clever bastards who's going to write a lot of stuff in the newspapers about how I'm facing the future with courage and determination. Well, foureyes, you've got it coming to you."

With this, he took the tray from his wife and with a gesture of infectious schoolboy fun smashed it over my head.

Slush

Yes, I thought to myself as I stumbled down the stairs wiping the cake crumbs from my wig. You can say what you like about Desmond Nit but you have to admire his courage and determination.

I *certainly* do. Don't you ?

DOCTOR FOOT'S
Child's Guide to Politics

OBEDIENCE *or A Member's duty*

DEMOCRACY *or Let the People Decide*

WORLD OF

BOOKS

The sheep has two legs

For the past six months, Professor Barbara Blacksheep has been living with a flock of sheep (Ovis Vulgaris) in the Neasden National Park. Her book THE SHEEP HAS TWO LEGS draws some profoundly disturbing parallels between the behaviour of sheep and that of Homo Sapiens. In this extract from her book, specially selected for serialisation in Private Eye, Professor Blacksheep describes some of the profoundly disturbing and ecologically exciting aspects of the sheep's sex life.

Like many young people in Britain and America today, the sheep is essentially promiscuous and enjoys sexual relationships with many different partners. Marriage in the human sense of the word is virtually unknown among sheep, a fact which casts a profoundly disturbing light on the whole idea of human monogamy, particularly when we recall that only 200 million years ago man himself was a sheep, swimming about in the primeval ooze.

I have observed many other profoundly disturbing parallels between the behaviour patterns of our two closely-knit species, such as the fact that the sheep often make a practice of wearing wool next to their skin. They also eat large quantities of grass, a substance closely related to many items in our own diet, such as the cabbage, cauliflower, rice pudding etc.

All we like sheep

Anyone who has observed the sheep at close quarters for many years, as I have, will eventually come to recognise the existence of what I have come to call the "Flock factor." This characteristic, which raises many profoundly disturbing parallels in human behaviour, can be observed, for example, when the sheep are frightened by a loud noise. The sheep will then band together in a troop, or "flock" as I have called it, and run off to another part of their pastoral environment, or "field" as it is known to ovologists.

He loves ewe - baa! baa! baa!

As I got to know my "flock" well, I came to recognise certain aspects of their daily behavioural life style which were even more profoundly disturbing. Each morning, for instance, the male sheep get up from their corner of the field, and after breakfasting on "toast" and "coffee," "drive off" to their day's work. The female sheep rise a little later and after cleaning out the pen and sending the young lambs off to their "play pen," wait eagerly with many a plaintive "baa" for the arrival of the milk-ram in his little electrically-operated float. Intimacy then takes place, lasting sometimes for four or five hours.

Meanwhile, many "black sheep," as I have come to know them, "drop out" of conventional flock behaviour norm patterns, and spend the day gambolling about, occasionally "smoking" a particular kind of "grass" which appears to give them hallucinatory sensations.

In recent years I have noticed a new and even more profoundly disturbing tendency in ovological life-patterns. Large numbers of the sheep have taken to retiring into secluded corners of their fields and writing long and profoundly disturbing books on the profoundly disturbing parallels between the behaviour of sheep and that of men.
Just where this tendency will all end, only many more years of research will indicate, but undoubtedly the results will provide us with some profound insights into the disturbing parallels which exist between ourselves and the animal kingdom.

T S Eliot's WASTE PAPER BASKET, with original contents, including notes and suggestions by EZRA POUND, MRS V ELIOT and MRS IVY MOPPS, in a limited facsimile edition of 800,000 copies (Gusset Press 47 gns).

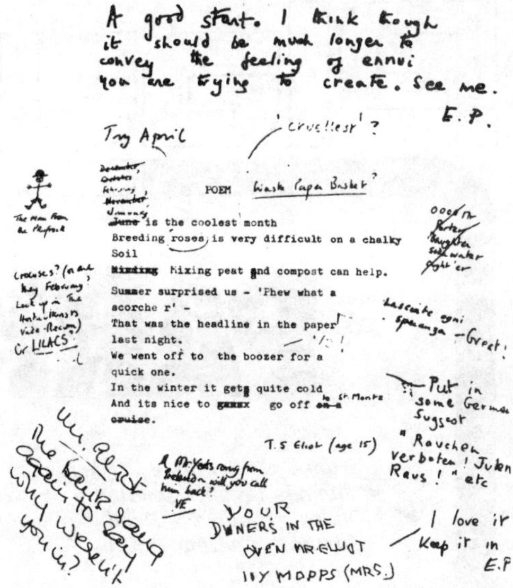

It is well-known that the original version of perhaps the most famous poem of the Twentieth Century was subjected by its author to severe cuts and emendations before appearing in the published form we know today. Now, at last, in this beautifully hand-woven volume, we can trace the springs of the creative process more clearly than in any other work since the notebooks of Beethoven were thrown into the fire by his absent-minded butler. In particular, the student of literature will be fascinated by the emendations suggested to Eliot by Ezra Pound (or Il Mille Miglia, as he is known to fans of grand prix motor-racing). We learn, for instance, that in his original version Eliot included a 23,000 word full-length parody of Dante's *Divine Comedy*, several extracts from the London telephone directory for 1921, the lyrics of a music hall song entitled *Arf a mo, guvnor, gor blimey, 'old yer 'air on* and a list of Huntingdonshire cabmen (with acknowledgements to J B Morton). All these Pound suggested Eliot should omit, on the grounds that they had been done before and much better by other authors. In their place, Pound added a number of stanzas of his own, including the gnomic extracts from the *Lal Bahadur Shastri* (or the Hindu Guide to Complete Satisfaction in Marriage) which have since attracted attention to the finished poem as perhaps the most seminal masterpiece in modern literature.

Playback

looks at TV topics that set you talking

PARKINSON'S

☆ *(Late night music. Parkinson bounds on with tousled hair carefully groomed. Producer waves arms. Audience claps.)*

Parkinson: Hello! Good Evening! Ee bah gum! And welcome to the show!

(Relaxes in executive-style black leatherex cum-steel-chrome chair. Gives sexy smile. 14 women carried out swooning.)

Parkinson: But seriously though, chums, I'd like you to meet one of the greatest names in cricket history, someone who's probably taken more wickets than most of us have had hot Lancashire puddings eh bah gum etc. etc. Ladies and gentlemen, it's the lad 'imself - Len Yobboe!!

(More music. Yobboe stumbles in. Producer waves arms. Audience claps. Parkinson pushes him into executive-style-black-leatherex-cum-steel-chair.)

Parkinson: 'Ow art then lad there's many a mickle makes a muckle taint there?

Yobboe: What's t'matter with thee? Don't tha know how t'speak proper like then lad?

(Uproarious laughter from audience. Parkinson smiles. Four more women faint.)

Parkinson: But seriously though, Lennie. A lot of people have said that the decline in cricket's popularity is due to the absence of characters like yourself.

Yobboe: Oh, aye.

Parkinson: The argument is that the game's deteriorated since colourful individualists like yourself were phased out by the faceless fuddy-duddies.

Yobboe: Oh aye. 'Appen.

(Loud laughter.)

Parkinson: Len, you are a legendary figure in the game and more stories are told about you than anyone since W.G. Parkinson.

Yobboe: You what?

(Renewed applause and laughter.)

Parkinson: The one I always remember was about you and Rev. David Shepherd ...

Yobboe: Oh aye. Mind you, I've always 'ad t'greatest respect and admiration for Rev. David Shepherd - after all, t'bugger's now some 'igh up sky pilot int' C. of E. i'nt 'e?

(Hysterical laughter.)

Anyway. It was t'Test. We was playing t'coons. *(Laughter.)*

Parkinson: You mean the West Indians?

Yobboe: Aye. That's right. T'cannibals.

(Mass hysteria breaks out. Renewed and prolonged applause and laughter.)

Yobboe: I was bowlin' last ball of t'over and this black bugger - they all look t'same to me - mind you Michael, I've got t'greatest respect for coloured folk. I've got fifteen of 'em livin' int' attic back home!!!

(Tears steam from audience's eyes. Two men dislocate arms whilst slapping thighs.)

Yobboe: Anyway, this bugger - Sobers, I think it was, snicked ball to Shepherd at

BAW

second slip. T'was easy chance only inch from t'ground six yards away from his left hand and t'bugger dropped t'bugger.

(Loud laughter.)

Yobboe: 'Old 'ard. 'Appen I've not finished tellin' t'tale.

Parkinson: What happened then, Len?

Yobboe: I shouted down t'wicket: "You daft sod! You've given sambo another bloody chance!"

(Audience breaks up furniture. Digitalis is issued freely by St. John's Ambulance men.)

Parkinson *(wiping tears from eyes)*: Well, *(sob)* I'm sure we're all agreed that this sort of thing is what cricket lacks today *(sob)*. And now ...

Yobboe: Eh, 'ang on. Wait for t'punch line. *(Nudges Parkinson. Winks.)* Punch line. Get it?

(Audience now on tenterhooks. A deathly hush falls.)

Parkinson: What happened next?

Yobboe: I runs down t'wicket and punches David Shepherd int' face. Punches 'im, see? 'E were unconscious for several seconds. Mind you, I've got t'greatest respect and admiration for David. After all's said and done, etc etc etc.

(Loud applause.)

Parkinson: Of course, nowadays all that fine old spirit has gone out of the game.

Yobboe: 'Appen 't'as, Michael, 'appen 't 'as. And more's t'pity ow't.

(Parkinson and Yobboe break into spontaneous weeping. Solemn music is played. Fade.)

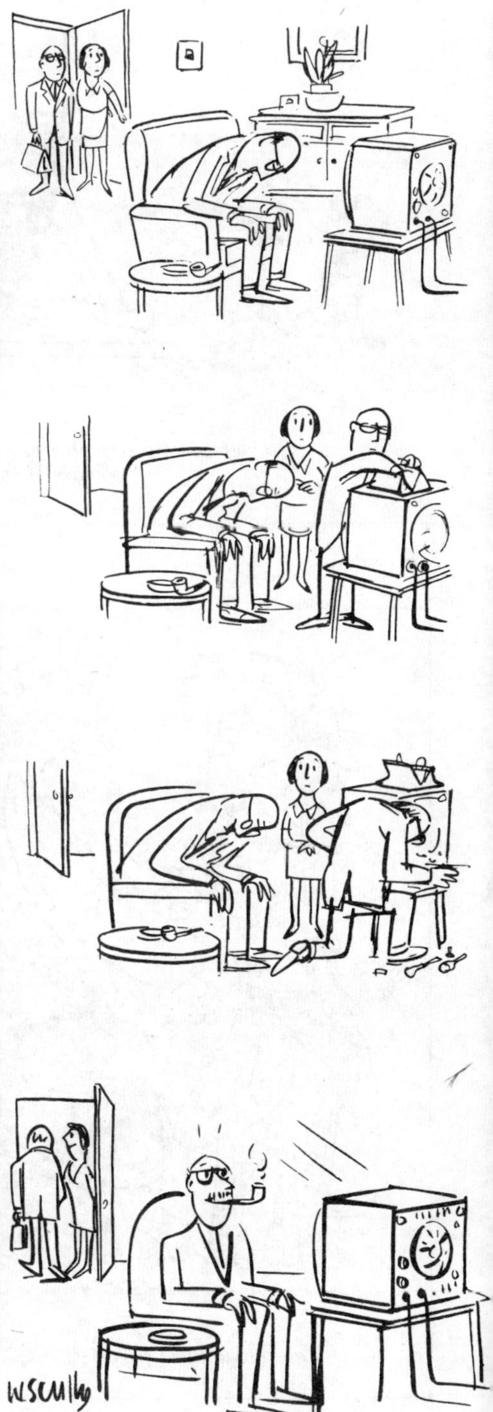

"Of course it's always been one of our basic premises that a happy treadmill is an efficient treadmill."

"Male chauvinist piglet!"

"If you want to know the time, ask a pig."

"You know what you got Nosher, you got class that's what you got"

"I say, is it frightfully warm, or is it just me ?"

Sports Standard

SOCCER

NEASDEN BEAT THAT JINX

By Our Man With The Police Escort

There were angry scenes at Neasden's Neasden Bridge Stadium on Saturday when fighting broke out between the two teams, Neasden and Tufnell Park Rovers.

Several players were taken to hospital and X Rays revealed that some of them may be out of the game for many years.

OFF SIDE

Trouble started when Referee Stan Trot from Upminster pointed to the centre after Terry Goals, the Neasden striker, had kicked a ball over the terrace roof.

Tufnell players surrounded the ref in protest but Trot firmly stood his ground indicating that a goal had been scored.

In the fighting that followed several players were injured and more Neasden goals were scored.

Said tight-lipped Neasden manager, Ron Knee, 59: "It was a great game to my mind. Terry took his goal beautifully. It was one of the best."

Asked to comment on the alleged blindness of referee Trot, Knee snapped: "This is fantastic to my mind. I have known Stan from way back. We are like brothers."

Further investigation revealed that this was indeed the case and that referee Trot is none other than Stan Knee, the refereeing brother of tight-lipped Neasden manager Ron Knee, 59.

SIZZLER

"It was great to see my lads amongst the goals" added Knee. "This is one in the eye for the knockers who said we were finished."

SCORE

Tufnell Park Rovers 0 Neasden 10

(Match declared void)

O'Relli transfer mystery

Knee denies "fiddle" story

by Our Man In The Directors' Box With A Little Something to Keep Him Quiet

Controversial Neasden soccer manager, Ron Knee, 59, last night angrily denied stories that he had obtained a five figure sum from Scottish club Queen of the Thistle in exchange for Neasden's hot property Italian-born long-haired Irish immigrant Bert O'Relli.

Said Knee, who last week moved into a new seven bedroomed house in Neasden's fashionable outskirts: "The deal is off, if it was ever on. As for my receiving money I am frankly astounded. O'Relli is one of the club's greatest assets. He is a youth with unique properties."

Transfer

But Thistle's tough-line manager Tommy

The Big Name Column **RON KNEE** of Neasden United

Knee gets tough

Controversial Neasden United manager, Ron Knee, 59, is to clamp down on the growing wave of policemen at the club's Neasden Bridge Road stadium.

Since the season started five weeks ago more than 50 arrests have been made at a cost to the club of well over £4, 000.

BOOT IN

Says Knee, 59: "I am sick to death of young coppers coming in here and breaking up the fun. They have no interest in the game and simply come along to make trouble."

There were startling scenes at Neasden Bridge only last week when soccer's Number One pin-up, Italian-born Irishman Bert O'Relli, was arrested during the second half of the match against Ongar Athletic.

O'Relli was charged with being in possession of an offensive weapon described as a length of lead piping which he had secreted in his shorts.

Police alleged that O'Relli had assaulted members of the Ongar team as a result of which large scale rioting had broken out on the pitch and police intervened.

PITCH BATTLE

Says 59-year-old Knee: "I am a man of few words. But our supporters and players come here for a good punch up. Football has come a long way from a lot of men kicking a ball about. Today it's a lot of men kicking each other about."

Mr Knee is 59.

LATE SCORE

Harlesden Wanderers 7 Neasden United 0

Jockerty tells a different story. "I want my cheque back" he snarled. "I have been swindled."

Says Knee, talking on the phone from his recently acquired Silver Cloud: "Football's a dirty game. It's tactics off the field as well as on that keeps a club ticking over."

Also ticking over was Knee's new chromatic shock-proof 79 jewel Swiss made self-winding wrist watch, as worn by men on the moon.

"Some of these Scottish clubs are a bit slow off the mark" he adds, "when it comes to kicking the ball around in the boardroom."

Punch Up

Not so happy were Neasden's faithful fans, hundreds of whom flocked to Neasden Bridge Stadium last Saturday to watch the home side play league-leaders Ongar Athletic.

But the match was abandoned when only two Neasden players turned up for the kick-off.

Violence broke out on the terraces and arrests were made. Said 59-year-old Knee, now holidaying in Spain: "It was a grand punch up. Who says soccer is dead when we can see fights like this for only a few shillings ?"

LATE SCORE

Ongar 7 Neasden 0
Match abandoned after 20 minutes

Your 12 x guide *by "Man O'The Pools"*

Fairlop Town	v. Dollis Hill Academicals X
Harlesden Wanderers	v. Arnos Grove 1
* Hatch End	v. Cockfosters FC 2
Tufnell Park Rovers	v. Neasden U 1
Kensal Green	v. Kilburn X

* Best Bet

Division 73 — Top placings

	P	W	L	D	Pts
Ongar Athletic	4	4	0	0	8
Harlesden Wanderers	4	3	0	1	7
Dollis Hill Academicals	4	3	0	1	7
Fairlop Town	4	3	1	0	6
Kilburn Rovers	4	2	1	1	5
Hatch End Hotspurs	4	1	2	1	3
Neasden United	4	0	4	0	0

Gnome Committee on Longford meets

"To hell with the fine weather! I'm eagerly waiting to be engulfed by this tidal wave of obscenity and pornography !"

Lord Gnome's Committee to investigate the possible harmful effects of Lord Longford met today at Gnome House.

The "Study Group", as it will be called, includes such well-known figures as the Bishop of Neasden, Basil Brush, the TV Personality, Mr Perishing Worthless, the Journalist and the Nawab of Twat, 43.

In his opening address, Lord Gnome said that as far as he was concerned his mind was closed to the subject of Lord Longford. In recent weeks it was impossible to open a newspaper without seeing Lord Longford, in one form or another, on almost every page.

There was no doubt that this caused widespread offence and could be harmful to the young. In his view, Lord Longford should be confined to the House of Lords, where he would be available on request only to bona fide researchers and anthropologists.

BISHOP'S PORN

Speaking for more liberal opinion, the Bishop of Neasden, Dr Trevor Muddledup, said it would be a pity if the Study Group were to acquire the image of a lot of old fogies and killjoys.

He personally intended to keep an open mind until they had examined Lord Longford from every point of view. Some people enjoyed Lord Longford, and he might well be a healthy safety-valve for dangerously pent-up emotions.

Mr Basil Brush said that he had worked in media throughout his career. People might be shocked or disturbed by Lord Longford at first sight, but familiarity induced feelings either of boredom or in his case, amusement.

"Lord Longford in himself," he told his audience, "is neither good nor bad. My children are so familiar with him now that they are simply bored."

The Committee then divided itself up into 49 sub-committees, each of which will study Lord Longford for several years and report back on their findings to a central "Thought Bank".

A 348-page report of the preliminary meeting will be published in the autumn and will be available under the counter at selected branches of W D and H O Smug, the Porn Merchants.

For the moment, in the days leading up to the official opening, the agenda has been dominated by politeness and protocol — and the noise of the workmen clearing up the Africans.

Grauniad

THAT DRESS - What a shocker!

Millions of viewers were stunned last night when film actress Rita Cadillac (46 - 28 - 46)appeared in front of Princess Anne (28 - 46 - 28) wearing controversial-style see-through hot-pants of the type that leave nothing to the imagination.

Miss Cadillac was being presented by the Princess with an award for her performance in the film *"The Landlady's A Bit of Alright."*

SHOCK

Viewers gasped as the little-known actress became better known in a couple of minutes as a result of her unusual clothing arrangements.

The Princess was visibly shaken as she presented the award but she managed to put a bold front on it, as did Miss Chevrolet (46 - 28- 46).

AMAZING

Miss Chevrolet said later: "I can't see what all the fuss is about quite frankly. The princess is a woman of the world who I am sure would not be shocked because Mother nature has dished me out with a king-size pair of boobies. "

Editor's note: Many readers may find parts of this story distasteful. We regret any distress which may be caused as a result of what they read.

We regard this story as a matter of considerable public interest and the fact that owing to the postal strike Mr Claud Cockburn's article has not arrived is in no way relevant to its inclusion.

Miss Chevrolet continued: "We have come a long way since Queen Victoria was shocked by the sight of a table leg. Royalty is with it these days, I mean you've only got to look at Lord Snowdon."

Laughing coarsely and winking Miss Chevrolet then posed for news cameramen.

A Buckingham Palace spokesman said last night that he would look into the matter closely. The Government is to set up an official enquiry.

Advertisement

Unbelievable

LÔÔK Its NEW!

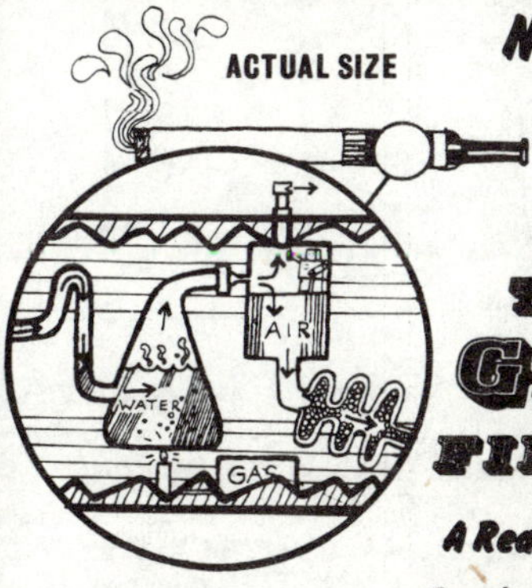

THE GNO FILTER

A Really Safe Smoke For Less Than 1p

At last for the millions of smokers for whom smoking is no longer a pleasure AN ENTIRELY NEW CONCEPT in the filter technique pioneered by top Swiss scientists working round the clock in the Bio-Gnome Laboratories at Lake Geneasden.

THIS amazing miracle in smoking technology guarantees you a dramatic 99%-style reduction in dangerous tars, gases, sulphurous fumes, nicotines, radioactive fall-out and other substances known to damage your health.

How it works.

A SCIENTIST EXPLAINS:

Each Gno-Filter contains a miniaturised laboratory complete with the very latest in up-to-the-minute scientific know-how guaranteed to reduce RISK to a bare minimum.

The smoke is drawn through the Gno-Filter into a series of tiny fibre-glass tubes where it is thoroughly processed, passing through WELL OVER A HUNDRED MILES of filter-tubing compressed into a container no bigger than a human three-penny bit.

From there, the smoke enters a tiny computerised "hydrometer" or water-filter. The water is kept boiling day and night by a minute Bunsen burner invisible to the naked eye. The steam forces harmful "tarry" smoke upwards into the "NO GRAVITY CHAMBER" where a microscopic robot propels it via charcoal-screens through tunnels back into the atmosphere.

MEANWHILE the by now SAFE-style smoke is gently eased through an aerated cooling-cushion, specially impregnated with neutralising GNOMA-NOXICHLORIFORMIOXYIOLIN (B^3), thus making it virtually harmless.

Will the GNO-FILTER reduce smokers' satisfaction ?

NO, say our scientists. The Gno-Filter operates without diminishing in ANY WAY the deep lasting richly-rewarding, strong, man-sized, navy-cut-style satisfaction that ordinary filter-free cigarettes give.

Only 1 new p for a packet of 5 filters

(+ £78 for Filter Holder)

Send now to GNOME INTERNATIONAL LABORATORIES, 38a Nightingale Mansions, Ongar, Middx (include s. a. e).

GNOMES LTD

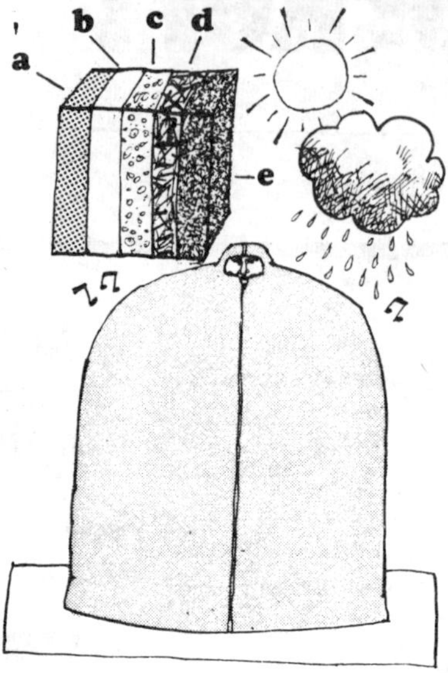

Decorating ? Gardening ? Motoring ? Fun-time ?

ALL PURPOSE COAT-STYLE MUSICAL COAT

Strong as a suit of armour YET light as a feather. Made in these FIVE thicknesses: (A) Windproof Gnomitex (B) Shock-proof Latex-style Neasdipillo (C) Aerated Tomalin (D) Dust-proof Fleecy-style Fibron (E) Water proof Wintex Triple-Style Lining. COOL in winter. HOT in summer. Plays "A Spoonful of Sugar" theme from Wagner's Tristan. Body-Temperature-operated. NEEDS NO WINDING.

HURRY! HURRY! HURRY!

IDEAL FOR MOTORISTS

Play it this Xmas

MOTORWAY MADNESS

the New Indoor Fun-Game For All The Family

All the thrills. All the Spills. All the Year Round Entertainment. A W H SMUG Game.

60% REDUCTION

GNOMEGA Ω

SAVE £106 TODAY

AMAZING MUSICAL

Unrepeatable .....

It actually TELLS the time!'. No more dials, hands or numbers. This Swiss-style revolution in time-telling SPEAKS the time. Operated by a microscopic SOLAR battery, this incredible no-need-to-look-at- it time piece is a must for everyone. Say Goodbye to Night Time frustration. Hear the time 24-HOURS-A-DAY. Sounds just like RADIO ONE. Dust - Wind - Water - Shock - Proof. Be like the Astronauts. Plays Pevsner's theme from "Woodcutter in the Alps."

£289 ... Money back Guarantee

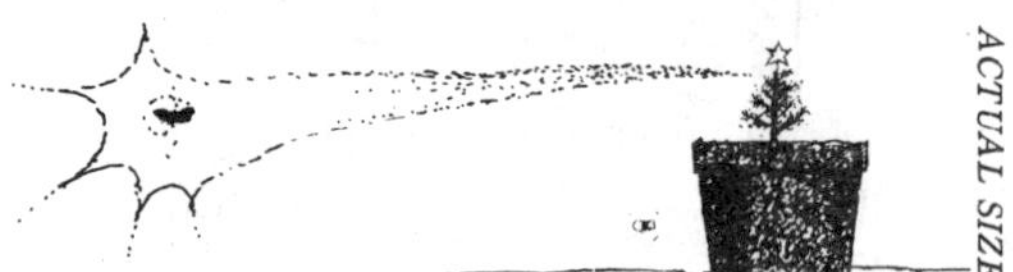

ACTUAL SIZE

THE PLANT FLIES HATE

Amazing LIVING Miniature Japanese-style Banzai Christmas Tree. Only 3" high. Must be seen to be believed. All flies die when bought into contact with the tree's invisible death rays.

OF NEASDEN

IDEAL FOR MOTORISTS

MAKE THE MOST OF YOUR CAR

More and more motorists are converting their unused space to make split-level travelling a reality for the 70s. A brand new idea that gives much needed EXTRA room for luggage, leisure-items or children. Also we advise the Professional Man. Write or Phone NOW for FULLY-ILLUSTRATED brochure. AUTO-ATTIC LTD, Pevsner Parade, Ongar.

LOOK

LAUGHTER TIME

Drive your friends crackers with musical <u>rubber</u> NUTTI-NUTS!! Watch them as they try to break a rubber nut. Hours of laughter. Ideal for Xmas Day and Year Round Entertainment. Plays "Climb Every Mountain" from Sound of Music.

AT LAST!!

NOVELTY CHOCOLATE SOAP

Good-bye
Bathtime Blues!

Your kiddies will LOVE this revolutionary idea in toilet novelty from LAVA-CHOC the Chocolate Soap People. Completely SAFE. Soap that you can ACTUALLY EAT!! All your favourite tastes and colours. (Also with LIQUEUR-CENTRES for Adults).

PARIS-INSPIRED MUSICAL
NAU-TEE-VEST
from Gaywear

Novelty Fun-style Undergarment. Warm, fluffy, body-hugging nylon vest with provocative cut-a-way see-through sau-cee Navel Display-Vent. A gay and frothy creation in fun-time colours: *Tame Tangerine*, *Passionate Puce*, *'Orrible Orange*. Plays Selections from the Merry Widower.

MUSICAL Leatherette-Style MOTORISTS'
ELECTRIC GLOVES

No More Cold Hands At The Wheel. Simply Plug In and Gloves Build UP Body-Temperature Warmth. Plays Lara's Theme from Dr Zhivago. Sky Blue. Ford Fawn. £4.99.

The Whitehouse Muggeridge Letters

Private Eye has acquired the world rights to this historic correspondence between Mrs Mary Whitehouse and Mr Malcolm Muggeridge

Dear Malcolm

Thank you so much for your lovely letter. I'm sorry I haven't replied sooner but since the autumn TV schedules arrived I've been busy going through them with a fine tooth comb looking for likely programmes to watch out for.

Incidentally I read your letter in today's *Daily Telegraph*. I do so agree as always with the sentiments you express. People do have this idea of me as a sort of old witch!! But, dear Malcolm, you at least realise what I'm really like, i.e. an ordinary housewife who leads a normal healthy life in every way.

I have just come back from a walk through the fields nearby. Don't you find that nature is a beautiful thing and brings you close to God ? It's difficult not to feel sad at autumn time as the leaves wither and fall. But I always try to think of spring, when the fields will be full of little lambs once again.

Talking of lambs, I'm afraid I cannot go all the way with you with your views about vegetarianism. Eric and I sampled the brazil nut cutlet you sent with your last letter but I confess we neither of us can see it as a permanent replacement for the old meat and two veg!! I do like a nice juicy steak now and again. Incidentally, I have never suffered from irregularity in my bowel movements. Perhaps this is largely due to my exercises which I do religiously every morning with the radio after my prayers and I am sure these also help me to lead an active sex life within the sacrament of marriage. Do you do exercises ? If you are interested I can send you a little book which is very easy to follow and sets them all out with diagrams.

With kindest thoughts,
Mary Whitehouse.

P.S. Did you see Tuesday's edition of *The Victims* ? It made my blood boil particularly the scene in the Moroccan prison. Perhaps you don't get it on Southern. Anyway, I have written to Lord Hill and copy to Frank (Longford).

Dear Mary

What a joy it was to get your letter this morning. How very observant you are about nature! I often go for long walks myself.

How sorry I am the nut cutlet did not meet with your full approval. Never mind. When we meet at the Cliff Richard rally next Wednesday I'll bring with me a box of herbal biscuits made from wheat germ and molasses which you can have a go at.

I do admire the way you keep plugging away at those BBC people. I'm afraid that as I get older I find the prospect of watching that little screen, which for me is far more frightening than the hydrogen bomb more and more distasteful.

Do tell me about your talk with the Pope. I would like to know what you made of the old boy.

Yours,
Malcolm Muggeridge

Dear Malcolm

Thank you ever so much for your letter. What a wonderful Saturday it was! I'm certain in my mind that the Festival of Light is the beginning of something and that from now on the BBC will really have to sit up and take notice!

Everyone I spoke to with one heart agreed that the Cleaning Up of TV programmes was so important for a really healthy society. Incidentally, one of our members in the Widnes branch, a dear old colonel who is now bedridden, wrote to say that he had seen the news coverage of our Festival and that they had done their best to play it all down and try to make it look as if there was only a handful of people in the square and not the thousands of happy wholesome young faces that you and I saw gazing up at us on the plinth. I have written to Lord Hill (copy to Charles Curran) drawing his attention to this bias. If you have a moment would you write as well, as I know your word counts a lot with the big brass at the "Beeb."

I have been out walking again and there is a real whiff of autumn in the air, isn't there ? D'you get the feeling like I do that God is in the trees and helping the spiders to spin their webs. I had a strange thought today as I walked down past Parsley Farm. I thought how like the seasons life is. I mean that winter is death and in the spring we come to life again with the daffodils. Have you ever thought this ? (I keep a little diary of thoughts like these. Eric finds them very helpful).

Thank you for the wheatgerm biscuits. They were a bit hard and broke my upper plate but apart from that they are very tasty. I am sure you are right about them being healthier than ordinary biscuits. By the way, did you see *Tomorrow's Laboratory* on BBC 2 last Wednesday ? Apparently in America someone has definitely proved that certain foods are harmful. But Eric and I say a pork sausage never hurt anyone!!! I know you won't agree.

I enclose some snaps Eric took in Trafalgar Square. I love the one of you with a pigeon on your head.

Eric says it reminds him of St Francis.

Goodness me, look at the time. It's time for Vice Squad. Do you get it on Southern ?

With my fondest regards,
Mary (Whitehouse)

Dear Mary

So our prayers for the rally all came true. I am sure as you so rightly say that it is the start of something, though of quite what precisely none of us can know. How marvellous to see so many hundreds of thousands of young people standing up to be counted.

As I get older I become increasingly aware that the younger generation is solely concerned with promiscuity and pot. It is infinitely depressing to see so many hundreds of thousands of young people, long-haired and pallid, obsessed by Sex in all its most degrading forms.

Thank you so much for the photographs. You still haven't told me about your visit to the Pope. I am dying to have the low-down. If you are writing to him again, do tell him what a good turn out we had. I'm sure it will cheer the old boy up.

Enclosed is a sachet of Sage and Cucumber Tea. You and Eric give it a try.

Yours afftntley
Malcolm M.

Dear Malcolm

Isn't the weather heavenly ? I have been out in the woods with Scrap (our little terrier) and to see the trees all red and gold like the sunset reminds me that Life can be beautiful and not dirty and nasty as it is so often portrayed on the BBC.

I have been meaning to consult you about the Common Market. Where do you take your stand in the Great Debate, Malcolm ? You see it seems to me that so much of this dirty material is flooding into our country from Europe and that if we get in, we will be able to do something about it. Do you agree ? I would so much welcome your view as I think on these political subjects your judgement is so much better than mine!!!

Incidentally I think the Pope agrees with me about the Common Market. I have sent him all our literature and I had a very nice note back from Cardinal Profumo thanking me and saying the Holy Father is "most sorrowful at the plight of our Catholic brethren in Ulster." I also asked if His Holiness would agree to become an Honorary Vice President of VALA but the Cardinal does not mention this in his reply. I have written again enclosing some of the preliminary reports of Frank's committee including the statistics from Pastor Branstrøm about bestiality in Finland.

Dear me! Look at the time. I must go or I shall miss *Murder Inc.*

Yours most affectionately,
MARY.

Dear Mary

Thank you so much for your letter. I saw Frank yesterday in the Dog and Bottle and gave him all your messages. The old boy has taken a tremendous shine to you.

As for this Common Market business, I find that as I get older I become more and more convinced that civilisation as we know it is doomed. Common Market or not Europe is spiritually bankrupt and it cannot be long before the Dark Ages come again.

Personally they cannot come soon enough!

Yours,
MM.

A *Spike Milligan* JOKE

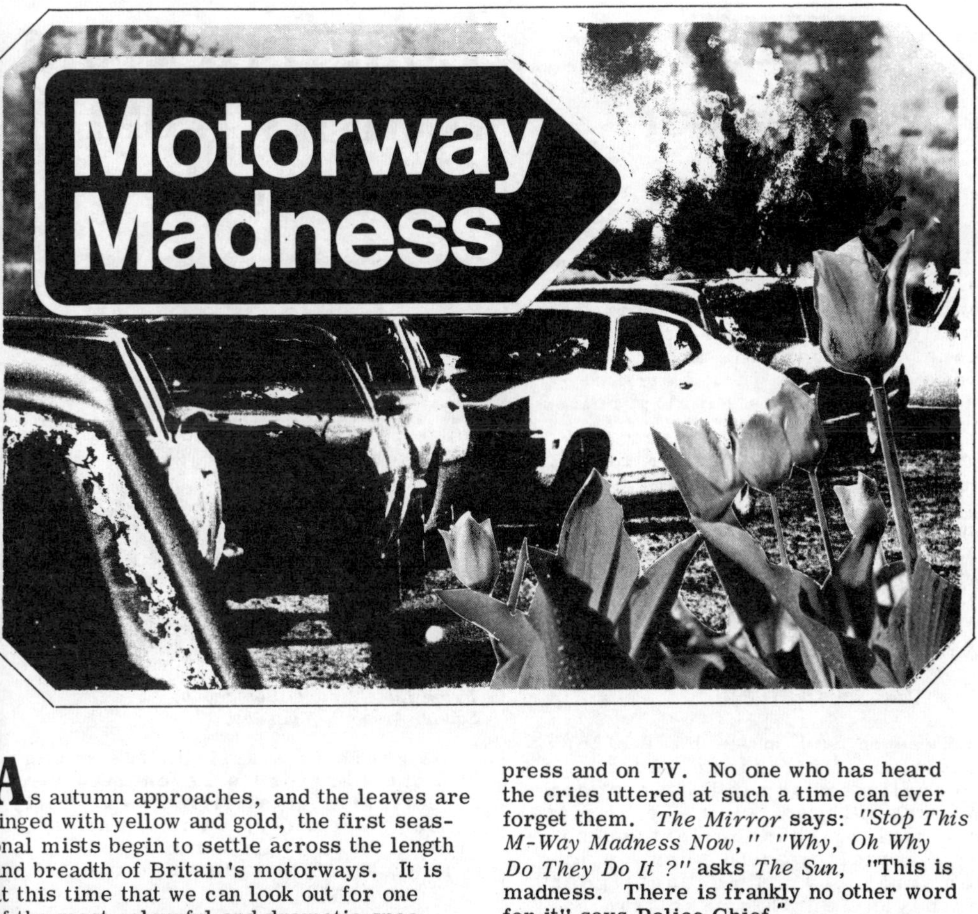

As autumn approaches, and the leaves are inged with yellow and gold, the first seas- nal mists begin to settle across the length nd breadth of Britain's motorways. It is t this time that we can look out for one f the most colourful and dramatic spec- acles of the English calendar - the Coming f the Motorway Madness.

As the patches of fog grow thicker, mot- rists from hundreds of miles around begin o gather, in long streams of vehicles of very shape and kind, from the tiny three- heeler to the gigantic articulated lorry.

Then, with flashing lights and sounding orns, the vehicles all plough into one nother at great speed, causing the cele- rated "multiple pile-ups," in which many housands die or are seriously injured.

This is the signal for a tremendous 'outcry" which lasts for several days, in the press and on TV. No one who has heard the cries uttered at such a time can ever forget them. *The Mirror* says: *"Stop This M-Way Madness Now," "Why, Oh Why Do They Do It ?"* asks *The Sun*, "This is madness. There is frankly no other word for it" says Police Chief."

The cry is next taken up by the "leader writers," many of whom propose ingenious methods whereby the "madness" could be avoided in the future. Some urge more flashing lights to warn motorists of the presence of fog, others that drive-in psychiatric clinics should be provided at every service station.

Within a few weeks, however, the up- roar dies away.

The darkness of winter descends and once again the "pile-ups" have become a regular, much-loved part of the traditional English winter scene.

The Sodom

THE INDEPENDENT NEWSPAPER

OPINION

The danger for Sodom

It is easy enough to poke fun at Lord Longford. In recent months his increasingly bizarre public activities and pronouncements have perhaps attracted more than their fair share of ridicule in the national scrolls.

Nevertheless, whatever may be thought of the manner in which Lord Longford is conducting his enquiries, we should not allow ourselves to be distracted from the underlying question at issue: Do we want the conditions currently prevailing in Gomorrah to be imported wholesale into Sodom ?

Sodom all

Here in Sodom we have a long tradition of tolerance and a generally broadminded approach to most things. But the climate of complete abandonment which has been allowed to grow up in Gomorrah, by all accounts goes far beyond anything that the average Sodomite would consider clean or natural.

Lord Longford's whole-hearted condemnation of what he has seen in the 'other city of the plain', will find an echo in the heart of every decent scribe and Pharisee in Sodom.

TALKING POINT

"Repent Ye Now."

Lord Beaverbrook

Longford team returns from Gomorrah

From Lunchtime O'Boolzebub, Sodom Airport, Tuesday.

Rumours of a split in the ranks of Lord Longford's seven-man sex investigation committee were hotly denied yesterday, on the team's arrival back from a fact-finding tour of the 'permissive paradise' of Gomorrah.

Said Longford: "Naturally we have our disagreements. But to say that we have not been on speaking terms for several days is an exaggeration of the truth."

Lot of rubbish

The seven-man team spent ten days touring the 'red-lamp' district of Gomorrah to see for themselves the effect of the 'anything goes' policy, which has made Gomorrah one of the main tourist attractions of the Middle East.

Earlier there had been reports of an incident at the 'Adam and Eve' Paradise Club, when two completely naked young

Times

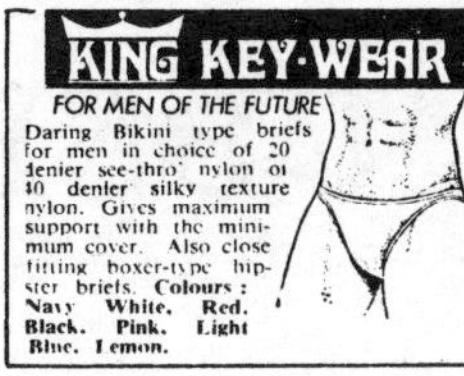

Gomorrhans offered Lord Longford an apple, which they said would bring about 'hallucinatory sensations.'

They then invited him to join with them in a 'happening' involving a giant 6 ft. python. Lord Longford left saying that he was 'deeply shocked,' and the naked couple were later ejected by the proprietor of the Paradise Club, a Mr G. 'Edgar' Hovah.

Kindly Eve the stage

Younger members of the committee, however, stayed on for several hours to see the rest of the show, and claimed later that they had been 'completely bored' by the whole experience.

Said 14-year-old Gyles Badbreath: 'There is a lot to be said for the Gomorrhan approach to sex. They have it all out in the open, so there is no guilt.

"According to one sociologist we met, since the abolition of sex laws, sex-crimes of all kinds have virtually disappeared'.

Sex Commandments

Another dissenter, Pere E Greene-Worthless, S.T., told how he had been so 'disgusted' and 'repelled' by everything that he had seen during his ten-day intensive study of Gomorrah's dirty-book shops, that he was all for introducing the same system into Sodom.

'Only by looking at filth like this can people come to appreciate the true value of love and marriage,' he said.

On other pages

'Brimstone ahead' say Met Men

The latest long-range forecast predicts the hottest day for Sodom since records were kept. The day may come any time in the next month, say weather prophets. Rainfall will be about average for the time of year, but freak fire-and-brimstone conditions may set in unexpectedly at any time. These could lead to widespread damage.

Festival of Lot

Over two people are expected to attend a mass-rally which is to be staged at the Royal Abraham Hall next month, to 'bear witness to purity'. The rally, organised by the Sodom League for Decency (Chairman Mr E Lot, Secretary Mrs E Lot), has been called in order that 'the just men' of Sodom may 'stand up and be counted'. When the 'just men' last stood up for this purpose, the score reached a total not higher than two, namely Mr and Mrs E Lot.

Mr Lot, a well-known member of the Sodom Community, has been described in the local press as 'the salt of the earth', and 'a pillar of society.'

Chess Corner No.1138769

Today's Problem: White. Porn to Bishop 2. Black to Mate (in public. Knacker swoops. Two Held).

Births

And Asa begat Josaphat: and Josaphat begat Joram: and Joram begat Ozias:

And Ozias begat Joatham: and Joatham begat Achaz: and Achaz begat Ezekias:

And Ezekias begat Manasses: and Manasses begat Amon: and Amon begat Josias:

And Josias begat Mechonias and his brethren, about the time they were carried away to Babylon (cont p 94)

OBSERVER REVIEW

Did David Astor really exist?

by Prof H R Trevor Roper

For hundreds of years the followers of David Astor have claimed that he was "divine." Now, a recently discovered heap of old back numbers of the *Observer*, found blocking a drain in Blackfriars, London, by a group of freelance rabbis, has shed astonishing new light on the Astor myth.

It seems that, far from being a "divine person," Astor was simply an ordinary man, little different from many other "preachers" of his day. The moral teachings which have for so long been associated uniquely with his name - the belief in the brotherhood of man, racial equality, peace, tolerance and progress - were in fact borrowed by Astor from many other thinkers of the time.

Mon-Astor-Schism

It seems clear from contemporary sources, such as the celebrated British Railways Rolls (a pile of mysterious rock-like substances found mouldering in a jar under the ruins of Sirjohn-bet-j'eman), that far from being one of the leading figures of his day, Astor was merely one "preacher" among many.

There were other, much better known prophets holding forth each Sunday to the eager congregations of the time, such as the notorious Muggeriah of Robertsbridge. The Muggeriah, who had a following of millions, roamed the Britain of those far-off days, eating only honey and crystallised locusts, preaching the imminent end of the world.

From the little we know of Astor, his preaching normally took the form of "leaders," long discourses to his followers in which both sides of a question would be examined impartially, concluding with a general call for moderation by all concerned.

So much for the historical evidence, scanty as it is. But are there not grounds, the responsible historian must ask, for going even further ? Was Astor a historical figure at all ? Or at least if he did exist, was he really such a holy man as legend would have us believe ?

Also Sprach David Astor

There are good grounds for suggesting that he was in fact a coloured sex pervert married to a lesbian drug pedlar living in Neasden. There are also good grounds for suggesting that he is the long-lost Astorovitch, heir to the throne of Russia, hitherto believed to have committed suicide in a bunker in Berlin in 1945.

Whatever the grounds may be, there seems no doubt that this kind of speculative rubbish will continue to fill the columns of the *Observer* Colour supplement for many years to come.

Next week: *How I Won The Election by Harold Wilson*

© Encyclopaedia Britannica 1971

COURT CIRCULAR

BUCKINGHAM PALACE

The Akond of Swat accompanied by the Akonda, the Prince Britvic and the Princess Ribena arrived in London this morning on a State Visit to the Queen and the Duke of Edinburgh at Buckingham Palace.

His Majesty and their Royal Highnesses were conducted to their carriages by Earl Fitzpestle (Master of the Balls) and accompanied by the Queen and the Duke of Edinburgh, drove to Buckingham Palace, a carriage Procession having been formed in the following order:

First Carriage

H M THE QUEEN
H M Mohammud Ali Habibullah Wazir Afewminitzago Werizi Now Yousihim Now U Dont, 14th AKOND OF SWAT

Second Carriage

H M Ayesha Hushpuppiz Launderama Metrogoldwyna Meir (The Akonda of Swat)
Field Marshal Hashish El Delhitelegraph (Grand Vizier & Master of the Imperial Umbrella)
Lady Angela Fitzalan Tightly (Lady-in-Waiting)
H R H Duke of Edinburgh

Third Carriage

H R H Idris Mazzawatte (The Prince Britvic)
His Excellency Lord Goodman
A. Wog (Keeper of the Imperial Purse)
Marquess of Smallbrain (Master of the Queen's Bathroom)

Fourth Carriage

H R H The Princess Ribena
The Princess Marie Louise von Tractatus-philosophicus von Wittgenstein.
Insp. Trimfittering
The Nadir of Pring
Lady Amnesia Spluttering (Mistress of the 7th Lord Bogside 1873-1945
H R H The Royal Photographer of Restricted Growth
The Arthur of Aski
Mr Eric Morley (Chairman: Mecca Dancing Limited)

First Motor Car .

The Viscount Gnome, PC, KCMG, ITV, NTBR
Very Rev Marty Carter-Ruck (Chaplain Extraordinary to the Royal Household)
Mr Kenneth Rose
Brig. Fakir Nawful Boxwallah (Commander in Chief, the Royal Swats Guards)

Second Motor Cycle

Inspector "Naqir et El Yard" Naqir (Royal Bodyguard)

Third Bicyle

The Lord Chancellor of Great Britain, the First Baron Hailsham of St Marylebone in the County of Herefordshire, PC, KG, MVO, NBG etc

Pogo Stick

Dr Yehudi Mazdah (Physician in Ordinary to the Akond of Swat)

On Foot

Citizens
Attendants
Soldiers
Serving Women
Protesting Students
Mr Ron "Badger" Hall
Heralds
Courtiers
etc

1427..BLAST OFF....1501..TAXI RENDEZVOUS....1629..H

NEASDEN 14

ATTERJI AND PERCIVAL RENDEZVOUS WITH KNOSE TCRTS...

IT'S ALL SYSTEMS GO FOR BLAST OFF!

Millions of scientists working round the clock at Gnome House are confident that the Lord Gnome three-man expedition to Neasden will "blast off" on schedule at 14.27 hrs (Neasden time) tomorrow.

Countdown has started at the Neasden Centre and there are no forseeable hitches. The captain of the Gnomi-naut team, Lt "Stuffy" Knose told a press conference last night that he was "looking good."

TENSION

If all goes well the three-man team will be in Neasden by Thursday.

This is the programme they will carry out:

1427 Blastoff from Gnome House. The team "walk" from Gnome House and attempt to get taxi to Tottenham Court Road tube station.

1501 Taxi-rendezvous plan jettisoned. Expedition proceeds with Phase 2 via London Transport bus. Room for one only on top deck. Lt Knose boards LTB. Takes seat in upper deck. Other two team members, Sgt. Maj. Hatterji and Lance Corporal Percival proceed on foot.

1629 Hatterji and Percival rendezvous with Knose TCRTS (Tottenham Court Road Tube Station). Owing decimalisation changeover ticket machines temporarily defunctionalised. Hatterji attaches himself to ticket queue while others purchase confectionery and evening papers from W H Smith.

1743 TCRTS escalation manoeuvre to lower level. LTB regret some delays to services owing to staff shortages and fog at Hainault. Knose boards "Speak your Weight" machine and relays information to base: "Machine out of order."

1820 Arrival of LT "Flying Cockfoster." Team link-up with train. Base contacts team with important news that they are off course. Knose re-diverted to Oxford Circus and Bakerloo Line.

Thursday

0013 Touchdown Neasden High Street. Gnomonauts rest procedure. Sleep-simulation.

0100 Team arrested for loitering by Neasden Flying Squad (PC Moonrock). Mission ends.

KNOSE, HATTERJI and PERCIVAL await blastoff in the tension-packed seconds before countdown at the multi-million pound Neasden centre at Gnome House. (Gnome-Press Agency Pic).

.1743..TCRTS ESCALATION....1820..ARRIVAL LT FLG COCK

NEASDEN 14

FOSTER....1972..NEASDEN UTD O KILBURN ROVS 13 DIV 73

These are the men

WHO WILL BRING YOU ROUND BY ROUND, SECOND BY SECOND, INFORMATION ON NEASDEN 14

Professor JODRELL BANK, 83. The Professor will monitor the early stages of Neasden 14 with his high powered binoculars - the largest in the world.

Dr PATRICK BOORE. Well known to Gnomevision viewers for his programme "Brush Up Your Stars," the Doctor will be installed in a GPO telephone booth fully equipped with new style decimal coin box and will keep viewers up to date with the latest test scores.

Computer "DAISY." All known facts in the world will be programmed and fed into this fabulous £800 million bundle of technical know how.

JIM BERK, 49. He is an expert in computer maintenance and will be telling viewers what is going wrong with computer "Daisy."

Weatherman SYBIL SLEET. Sybil is an expert in long-range weather-forecasting. She will interpret the weather conditions as and when they happen.

Dr LARRY SCHWEPPES, Professor of Advanced Neurosis at the University of Moosejaw, Mass. Dr Schweppes is a leading authority on how human beings react under extreme pressure. He will interpret the Gnomonauts' inner feelings as they voyage hundreds of feet beneath the earth's surface at a speed of up to 20 miles an hour.

Comedian RON LAUGH will come along and tell jokes when TV coverage of Neasden 14 breaks down due to wildcat strikes.

WHY NEASDEN 14? asks Patrick Boore

There was mounting criticism in recent weeks of the latest Neasden probe from people who question the expenditure of large sums on what seems to the outsider a pretty pointless exercise.

The critics say that there is nothing new to be learnt by going to Neasden yet again. The earlier expeditions, they say, have told us all we need to know about this bleak and inhospitable wasteland.

Certainly we scientists have learnt a good deal from previous probes. We know, for example, that there is no life there, at least life as we know it. But we still do not know when or how Neasden came into being. Did it for example, break off from Willesden millions of years ago, or was it once a part of Dollis Hill that has somehow drifted apart from the gravitational pull to have become a separate entity ?

This is what we expect to learn by Neasden 14. It is hoped that Lt Knose and his team will bring back specimens of Neasden rock from the hitherto unexplored King George VI Memorial Park. Though to the layman these objects look like boring old pieces of paving stone, such as you might find on the surface of the moon, to us scientists they are like nuggets of pure gold which may well contain the secret of Neasden.

The Jesus Freaks

by Our Religious Correspondent

A new craze is sweeping through Britain like a forest fire. After the Teddy Boys, the Mods and Rockers, the Hippies - now it's the Jesus Freaks.

Just who are these self-styled Jesus Freaks - the men and women who overnight have caught the imagination of journalists like myself with nothing better to do.

The Young Mitres

The Freaks follow the teachings of a 33-year-old Jew who died in Palestine 2000 years ago.

"A lot of us feel don't we" says one Freak in the typical jargon employed by the cult-followers "that there's more to life than just, you know, having a good time and all that sort of thing. It's only too easy isn't it just to jog along without thinking of higher things. But you know many people today, particularly young people are looking for something outside themselves. I often think that life is like a ride on the railway. Some of us get a first class ticket and some of us get a third. But we all have to get off in the end. I think that's awfully true don't you ? Would you care to join my wife and I in a glass of this delicious Neasdillado sherry ? It's a little on the sweet side I'm afraid."

The speaker is Michael Ramsey, self-styled "Archbishop of Canterbury" - a quaint name used by the Freaks to describe their leader.

With his long fuzzy white hair, rings, necklaces and flowing ground-length Kaftan-style robes, Ramsey cuts a bizarre figure.

Carnaby Heenan

But there are other people in the movement who make Ramsey seem as conventional as a bank manager on his way into work.

One such is "Mad Frank" Pakenham, who sometimes calls himself the Earl of Longford.

Longford, a balding, wild-eyed eccentric, belongs to the extremist "wing" of the Freaks and describes himself as a "Roman Catholic."

Unlike Ramsey, "Loony" Longford is an activist, convinced of his messianic calling to change the world.

Says Longford, gesticulating wildly and pacing the room in a long flowing macintosh: "Like man, this whole spooky world is too much man. The whole pornography scene is a bad trip. Like cats should dig the Good Book not the dirty book because that scene is way out and Jesus saves if you dig me. Like would you care to partake in a glass of this too much sherry man. Like it grooves you in on a swinging scene."

Lord Longford is old enough to know better.

Dr Gnome's Health Sandal

Beware of Imitations

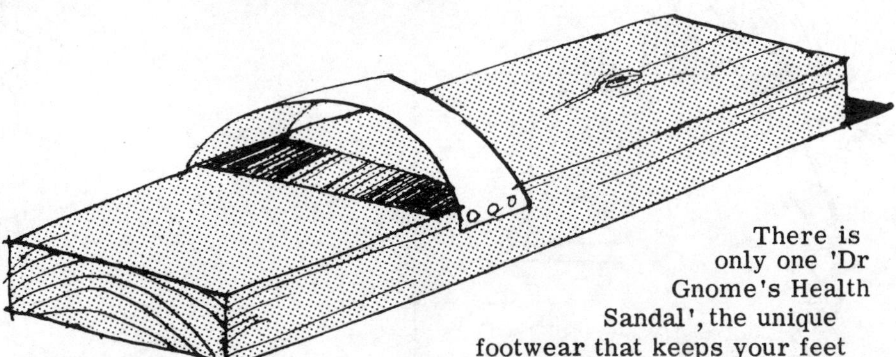

There is only one 'Dr Gnome's Health Sandal', the unique footwear that keeps your feet in tip-top condition as well as prolonging active sex life.

You can tell the Gnome Sandal by its hand-tooled contours designed to caress the natural shape of the human foot. Look for the Dr G Symbol and the £20 price tag - sign of authenticity.

From all stockists

"Listen, I can't do any more for you. You're goofy."

"Come on in, the waiter's lovely."

SOCCER

O'Relli cleared by FA shock verdict

by E I Addio, Our Man in the F A Disciplinary Committee room

A tired but triumphant Ron Knee, 59, emerged last night from the all-night sitting of the Football Association (Neasden branch) to tell reporters that Neasden hot property Irish-born Bert O'Relli had been officially "cleared" of charges of causing grievous bodily harm to referee Sid Himmler during the North Circular Relegation Trophy Match last May.

Said an ashen-faced Knee: "I feel tired but triumphant, despite my ashen face. Things have been looking black for Bert since the new "get tough" policy was pushed through by the referees in total opposition to the wishes of the clubs."

FINAL WHISTLE

The charge against O'Relli followed an incident in which it was alleged he had fired a gun at Himmler from close range with intent to kill.

The alleged shooting came after Himmler had "booked" O'Relli: for gross indecency involving Dollis Hill midfield dynamo, Jeremy Strangelove.

AMAZING RELEGATION

Last night an FA official said: "We are satisfied now that Mr O'Relli had not intended the bullet for referee Himmler.

"The fact that it struck Neasden chairman, Launderama magnate, Brig. "Buffy" Cohen as he sat in the directors' box with Polish-born Qantas air-hostess, Miss Roxana Dabitoff, is no concern of the FA."

Last night Brig. Cohen's condition was stated to be "ashen-faced" by a Neasden General Hospital spokesman.

LATE SCORE

Eurodent Inter-Suburbs Trophy (1st Round)

F A (Sanilav) 10 Neasden 0

Knee cracks down on ticket touts

by Our Man On the Terraces With the Nasty Cough

Controversial soccer manager, tight-lipped Ron Knee, 59, last night cracked down on ticket touts who failed to sell a single ticket for the forthcoming Inter Cities Cup Tie between Neasden and F C Limoges.

Said Knee: "To my certain knowledge some of these men have been out on the streets for days without making a single sale. With relegation staring us in the face, we cannot afford to miss a golden opportunity of this kind."

Substitute

But Neasden received a further shock when the FA disciplinary committee stepped in following newspaper disclosures about a "racket" in rigged tickets.

According to a newspaper report Neasden players have sold "Cup Final" tickets to unsuspecting tourists. But on closer inspection the so-called Cup Final turns out to be the North Circular counties Cup Final between Harlesden Rovers and Snaresbrook City.

Questioned about these allegations an ashen-faced Knee said: "My lads are strong athletes. Football is their bread and butter. They would never stoop so low. And if they did, who can blame them ? They have been under a lot of psychological strain recently especially young O'Relli who has been experimenting with hallucinatory drugs as a way of breaking his goal famine."

LATE SCORE

Neasden 0 FC Limoges 10

HAROLD WILSON

continues the astonishing story of his 'Unknown Years of Power.'
Part 81: How I Outsmarted Hitler and Averted World War Two.

'I fly to Munich'

I realised that there was something unpleasant about Adolf Hitler from the moment I saw his picture in the paper. I remember recalling this fact to my friend President Lyndon Johnson, when we met some years later in the White House. With typical Texan shrewdness, he agreed that he himself had always suspected that Hitler had been "up to no good."

It was late in the August of 1938 that I first met Herr Hitler face to face. As I had long imagined, he was a small, dark-haired man with a tiny bristling moustache, which reminded me vividly of Charlie Chaplin in the film *The Great Dictator*, which, when it was made some years later, I much admired.

When I arrived in Munich, I immediately invited Herr Hitler to join me for afternoon tea at the British Legation. To this day I recall sitting there, looking at my watch and waiting for the entrance of the most-hated man in the world.

By eight o'clock there was no sign of him. So I decided to fly in person to meet him at his mountain hideout.

'For the first time in my life I loose my temper'

I arrived at Berchtesgarden, the notorious bullet-proof bunker nestling at the foot of the Matterhorn, later that night.

I found Hitler alone in his study, putting the finishing touches to a little watercolour landscape, which was later to be described as "an exquisite and agreeable evocation of the spirit of twilight in the Bavarian Alps" by no less an authority than Sir Kenneth Clark, whom I was later personally to ennoble at the request of my wife, Gladys.

Hitler cringed at my entry. It was pathetic to see a man so obviously in awe of me. I banged my fist on the table, and produced from my pocket a copy of the famous so-called *Five Principles* which I had

jotted down on the back of my cheque book on my way over in the aeroplane.

They were as follows:

1. No invasion of the Rhineland.
2. No Anschluss with Austria.
3. No mass-extermination of six million Jews.
4. No invasion of Belgium, Czechoslovakia, Holland, France, Norway, Denmark, Greece, Russia, etc.
5. Unimpeded progress towards an unconditional surrender to my armies.

Hitler's face turned a deathly white as he read my terms. For a moment his hand shook. I fixed him with a steely glare. It was obvious he realised the game was up. "This is the end of the line, Adolf" I told him frankly. "Y'know, a thousand years in politics is a long time." A faint smile crept over the Fuehrer's face and he signed the document. It was the end of an era.

'I listen to Goering's dirty stories'

Later that night, I was the guest of honour at a reception given on the stage of the Opera House at Bayreuth. Amongst those present were Lyndon Johnson, with whom I was later to have many frank exchanges in the White House, His Majesty the King, father of our present Queen, with whom I was later to stay on a number of occasions at Balmoral Castle and elsewhere, Lord Cromer, the founder of modern Egypt, and Sir Robert Menzies, whom I have always thought of as the Father of the Commonwealth.

Of course, in the light of later events, my diplomatic victory over Hitler was widely misunderstood. The Opposition was to allege that it was wrong of me to let Hitler know in advance that I completely ruled out the use of force. It is true that the outbreak of World War II in 1939 did much to encourage the critics of my Munich policy into thinking that I had failed and that Hitler was insincere in agreeing to my Five Principles. But the fact remains that had it not been for the coming of the war, I would have been unable to inspire the British people through the perils and tribulations of the six long, dark years that lay ahead.

NEXT WEEK
- *Dunkirk - my finest hour*
- *Few! What a Battle of Britain*
- *George Brown gets cold feet*
- *How I won El Alamein*

THE ARTS

Bacon retrospective

by Our Art Correspondent

EDWARD LUCIE-PSEUD

Huge areas of bloated pink flesh, dripping blood onto the floor below. Guts spattered on marble slabs. Old men bent double under shapeless carcases, their faces contorted into silent paradigms of effort and agony. Grey, sinister metal cleavers, frozen in the act of hewing limb from limb.

The raw primal impact of the gigantic Bacon exhibition, currently on show at Smithfield Market this week, is enough to take one's breath away. Even to walk into the great gallery is a chilling experience in itself (owing to the deep-frozen temperatures at which the exhibits are preserved).

Surely here we have the most nightmarish vision of our times that the twentieth century has produced. The stench of death, the blood-splashed pavements, twisted, tormented corpses, sinister echoes of Auschwitz and Dachau - these are just some of the phrases which it is *de rigeur* for anyone reviewing this exhibition to throw in from time to time.

Agonising

Centrepiece of this staggering show is the vast carcase of a boar, spreadeagled on a row of meat hooks in an image that reminds one not only of Belsen but of the crucifixion, not only of Grunewald but of Eisenstein, not only of Hiroshima but of Enoch Powell in the pose of some gigantic boar, spreadeagled on a row of meat hooks in an image that reminds one etc.

In contrast to this gargantuan icon of suffering, the eye moves in relief to a series of delicate, exquisitely carved little rashers. With their beautifully modulated colouring in streaks of pink and white, the colours of life and death (or if you prefer it, of lean and fat), they echo in a minor key the mighty discords of the vast carcases which hang in rows through the gallery on all sides. And yet one somenow feels that they too are only part of the whole - and that what we are seeing is a glimpse of the (cont p 94)

"WHERE THERE'S MUNCH THERE'S MONET"

NEWS IN THE ARTS

NATIONAL GALLERY TO SELL PAINTINGS SHOCK

by Our Salesroom Correspondent,
GERALDINE SOTHEBY-TIMES-INDEX

There is some disquiet in artistic circles about the decision of the Trustees of the National Gallery to send the gallery's pictures to auction at Sotheby's next week.

It is believed that the gallery's collection could well fetch a record sum for a sale of this kind, possibly running into many trillions of pounds.

One picture alone, Fra Olivetti di Lamborghini's *Landscape With Sir Kenneth Clark and Dogs* could fetch up to £1,000,000 according to art historian Lord Clark of Civilisation (repeat).

When the Titian had to stop

A gallery spokesman explained yesterday that the decision to sell off all the gallery's pictures, many of them priceless masterpieces known to art lovers the world over, had only been taken with the greatest reluctance.

"Unfortunately these are hard times for any art gallery and what with inflation and so forth, we have got to raise a very large sum of money to keep the gallery open at all."

24 Corot sold

The gallery's financial crisis has come to a head over the government's recent decision to impose admission charges. The cost of installing up-to-date turnstiles, the printing of tickets, and the recruiting of specially-trained male nurses to extract visitors from the turnstiles when they break down, has proved the last straw in the gallery's skyrocketing budgetary problems.

Critics of the scheme to sell off the paintings have been quick to point out that many of the gallery's most celebrated masterpieces, such as Constable's *The K Wain* (sometimes known as *Jumping on the Bandwagon)* and Kenaletto's *Very Agreeable View of the Grand Canal* (otherwise known as *Anyone for Venice)* and *The Clark Ascending* by Ralph Vaughan-Williams Williams *(Isn't there some mistake ? Ed)*

We interrupt this piece to bring you a late protest from a typical reader:

Dear Sir,

Like many of your readers I am getting (sic) and tired of these continual disagreable references to Lord Clark of Civilisation. It is surely only too easy to make fun of someone like Kenneth who is doing his best to bring the world's mast erpieces into the front rooms of ordinary people who would otherwise remain ignorant philistines spending their time on nothing better than bingo and football pools. If only one of these moronic individuals has been influenced by the series into putting aside his "coupon" and taking advantage of the "See Civilisation in Fourteen Days All-Inclusive Coach Trip" organised by Messrs Kenneth Clarkson Culturetours Ltd, Neasden, then it will have been worth every penny of the £285,000 which the programme cost to make.

I remain, yours agreeably
KENNETH 'NOBBY' CLARK
(the Man Who Put "K" Into Culture)
The Big House
Malby Crofton
Kent.

---

were left to the gallery in perpetual trust for the nation by many benefactors. It would therefore be illegal, such critics argue, for the gallery to sell the paintings. However, in the opinion of at least one eminent lawyer, Lord Shawcross, such bequests can readily be set aside by any determined gallery. "Never you mind, boy," Lord Shawcross told me yesterday. "Some of these geezers have been pushin' up the daisies since I don't known how long. I tell you, look at it this way, you don't get a high-class legal eagle like yours truly fiddling the small print when there's any risk of a comeback, already."

HOLIDAYS OF

Off the beaten track

with CYRIL LORD DAVID CECIL B. DE MILLE

Are you tired of those stereotyped holidays like crossing the Sahara on a pogo stick or climbing the Himalayas in a wheel chair ? So how about something really different this year ?

Just a stone's thrown from Kilburn lies a little spot which I bet you won't find mentioned in any travel brochure. It's completely unspoilt and while I was there I did not see a single tourist. Such a spot is only too rare these days when travellers have penetrated to almost every corner of the globe.

Where is it ? If you promise to keep it under your hat, I'll whisper it in your ear. Neasden. The name conjures up a fairly land, a Nirvana, a veritable Atlantis. And so it is.

How to get there

Why not travel leisurely overland in a bright red London transport bus. Or, if like me you want to get there quickly, go by what Neasden folk call the Tube. It's on the Bakerloo line between Dollis Hill and Harlesden. Or you can fly to Luton and take a taxi.

Where to stay

There is only one hotel and try as I might I could not find it in any guide book. Indeed, I could not find it at all. But perhaps you will be luckier. It is called The Neasitel - and has yet no star rating - a good omen, think I. (For all I know it may have been demolished in Neasden's extensive rebuilding programme which while I remember is a feast for anyone who likes looking at new buildings).

Take a walk down Neasden High St to Lovedales (Newsagent & Confectioners). They have an informative display of postcards bearing landladies' names and add-

A LIFETIME

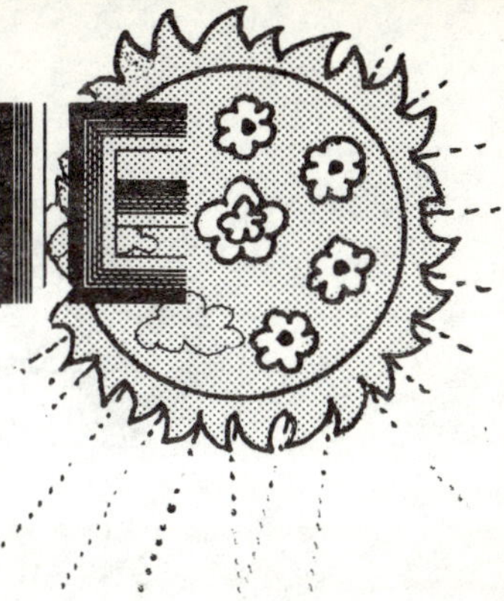

resses pinned up in their little windows. (I stayed with a Mrs Weidenfeld and her elder son in Elgar Crescent. The fare was plain but filling).

What to do

Take a stroll down Neasden High St and turn right at Millets (Neasden) into Selfridge Road. Pop in the Public Library and browse at your leisure in the many newspapers on display (9.30 to 4.30 most days). Then how about a drink at one of the many local public houses ? The Duke of Edinburgh (Woolworth St) serves the local Kilburn Ale.

Night Life

Eating out is an adventure. Try the Fiesta (Tesco Road) just by the station. Specialities: Egg and chipps 3s 9d. Egg, chips and peas 4s 6d. Egg chips sausage and peas 5s 6d. Egg chips sausage bacon and peas 6s 9d. Egg chips sausage bacon tomato and peas 7s 11d. Egg chips sausage bacon tomato beans and peas 8s 9d. Eggs chips sausage bacon tomato beans fried bread and peas 12s 6d.

The tea is local; rough and strong and full of leaves.

After supper why not stroll down to the brightly lit High St to the Lots Of Fun Amusement Arcade - where the elite of Neasden "have a flutter" at the many colourful machine games.

Bingo can be fun. And profitable too. They play it every Thursday at the Essoldo cinema.

Souvenirs

Take home Neasden-made hush-puppy style gloves (Millets 45s). Also canary-yellow cardigans with 'football' leather buttons. Everyone wears them in Neasden.

Bon voyage!

FIVE BID FOR GNOME AWARD

'A substantial sum of money to be awarded annually to that author who in the opinion of the judges writes the most hard-hitting, frank, outspoken, elusive, reticent, fastidious etc. etc. work of fiction to have been published in the past ten years"

So say the sponsors of the world-famous £5,000,000 Gnome Fiction Prize, to be awarded this year by a panel of judges which includes lovely young authoress and prominent society hostess Lady Magnesia Freelove, the philosopher and man of letters, Dr Jonathan Miller, novelist Margaret Drivel, Mr Eric Morley, Chairman of Mecca Dancing Ltd, and world-famous philanthropist and connoisseur of the arts, Lord Gnome. (12th man: Lord Clark of Civilisation).

The short-listed candidates for this year's Gnome Prize include:

1. Bhindi Ghosht, 49. A shy, elusive deeply-reticent man, Ghosht lives in a boarding house in Ongar. His only book, the widely-acclaimed *Languor in the Afternoon,* was first published in 1947. A shy, elusive, waif-like man of 26, he looks and sounds much older than his 52 years. "I feel very, very tired" he told me, when I rang him at 3 o'clock in the morning. Among the words he used freely were "annoyed, rude, trying to get some sleep, goodbye."

2. Mavis Twitting, 74. Alone of the six finalists, Miss Twitting refused to be interviewed. Her widely acclaimed trilogy *What A Way To Go,* is a deeply-sensitive exploration of the problems of a group of suicidally-inclined intellectuals living in Earls Court during the last 20 years. In a long letter, she writes to me: "Everything I have ever wanted to say is in my book, except what I am just writing to you in this letter, which is to say, stop pestering me with your silly questions. I have no interest in prizes, which are just to my mind part of the whole male chauvinist exploitation of the female sex, so just give me the money and leave me alone."

3. Moregetai Richer, 45. A shy, intensely-extrovert Canadian-Jewish intellectual, Richer gestures a lot with his hands and lives in a tall, gaunt Edwardian houseboat on the Staines Reservoir. The title of his new book, *The Four Just Men In A Boat,* by Jerome K Kern, took him over 14 years to think up. "Even now I am not quite happy with it" he says, in his shy, outspoken way. While writing his widely acclaimed masterpiece, Richer dashed off a pot-boiler *Porn Free,* which made him a millionaire. "I only did it for the money" he says in his shy, deeply reticent manner.

4. Millicent Reticent, 52. Perhaps the most reticent of all the finalists, she has not been seen by anyone for several years. Even her husband regards her as something of an enigma. "Millicent is intensely modest" he says. "She is not only very shy about her work but also so intensely self-critical that she has not as yet put pen to paper. If it is reticence and shyness the judges are looking for, then she is their woman. She is certainly not mine."

5. Lord Gnome, age not known. A shy, intensely elusive philanthropist and multi-millionaire, he is widely tipped by insiders as the favourite for the prize. His recently, widely-acclaimed novel *War and Peace,* a colourful drama of everyday life in Napoleonic Russia, was widely recognised as a masterpiece from the moment it was first published in 1869 under the pseudonym of "Count Tolstoy."

THE ANATOMY OF GNOME by Anatomy Sampson

(Extract reprinted by kind permission of Snipcock and Tweed).

Chapter Seventeen: POWER

"We cannot altogether resist the conclusion that those responsible for the direction of the Gnome Organisation have acted somewhat unwisely in this matter, but we can see no reason for any further action by Scotland Yard, the Monopolies Commission or the Director of Public Prosecutions."

Board of Trade Investigation Reports, 1959, 1962, 1966, 1971.

There could be no better illustration of the changes that have come over Britain in the past ten years than the mammoth £700 billion Gnome Organisation. In less than a decade, this abrasive, go-getting concern has risen from nowhere to become the dominant force in the commercial life of the country (with interests ranging from television rentals to motorway service stations, from pop records to pornography, from package holidays to switch-sale encyclopaedias).

The headquarters of the group, a gleaming, 58-storey, Seifert-designed tower in the go-ahead, Los-Angeles-style suburb of Neasden, conveys at once the mixture of abrasive meritocratic dynamism with suave, old-school tie assurance which in recent years has given the name of Gnome more column inches in the City financial pages than any other company of comparable size *(see Table 12)*.

Once inside the 41-foot bronze doors (a copy of Ghiberti's famous Florence Baptistry, personally chosen by Lord Clark of Civilisation) the visitor is whisked away into a dreamworld, in which the old jostles happily with the new. Grey-haired, silver-moustached Old Etonians with double-barrelled names rub shoulders with black-booted, velvet-shirted whizz kids in Tibetan-style kaftans designed by Mr Fish. Flash-neon Op-Art kinetic mobiles by Bridget Riley dazzle from oak-panelled walls hung with priceless family portraits from Harrods.

Some idea of the very real changes that have taken place within the Gnome group in recent years can be seen from the following table showing the percentage of Oxbridge graduates working in the packing department:

	1958	1969
Leisurewear	24	201
Roadholding capacity	16	11
Do-it-yourself	8	27
Redbrick	17	84
Don't know	100	100

At the centre of this gigantic web (with its tentacles stretching into five continents and even into Outer Space), sits the enigmatic figure of Lord Gnome himself. Gnome's background is mysterious. Believed by some to have been the son of a Lithuanian cocaine-smuggler, who immigrated to this country during the Estonian sauerkraut famine of the 1890's, he is said by others to have been born in a terrace house on the outskirts of Salford. A shy, retiring figure, who dislikes publicity (he is one of the two people who refused to grant me an interview for this book, except on payment of a £1000 fee), he spends much of his time abroad, delegating the day-to-day running of his companies to his immensely capable, Suffolk-born aide, Emmanuel Strabes. Gnome first sprung to public attention as the mysterious "Mr X" in the notorious Throgmorton blackmail scandal of the late 30's. Today he is undoubtedly one of the three most powerful men in the country. He has the ear of politicians, media-men, film stars and Soho villains alike. His amazing grasp of detail, his breadth of vision, his 24-hour-a-day telephone-answering service, his skilful deployment of the celebrated Cheapside legal firm, Sue, Grabbit and Runne to stifle any hint of public criticism all contribute to make him undoubtedly the most fascinating, dynamic, abrasive personality in British business today. And yet it would be a mistake to exaggerate his importance (cont p 994)

"It's his old steam radio."

"It's the butler who gets screwed!"

"I hope you are not going to engage me in conversation."

"Not while I'm on duty Sir."

The Press

NEW OVERGROUND PAPER ON SALE

by Sid Caesar Augustus John Neville Chamberlain

A new "overground" paper called *The Daily Mail* is currently appearing on various bookstands in London and elsewhere. Its aim, according to its editor Mr David English, is to "bridge the gap" between the *Daily Sketch* and the *Daily Express*.

"Basically" says English, "our object is to print all those stories which don't get into the underground papers."

BALLS

The new paper is the latest in a long line of "overground" papers, all of them claiming large circulations and committed to the "alternative society."

One of the most successful "overground" papers is the so-called international *Times* edited by bespectacled eccentric William Rees-Mogg (or Moggy as he is known to his "groupies," men like Charles Douglas Vass, another drop out from upper-class nonconformity.)

CROSSWORD

The readers of the *Times* says Mogg, are "main-liners" - that is, people who travel to and from London by train.

"Yes, they are easily recognisable with their short hair and bowler hats. The underground press has given them a bad image but basically many of them are simply looking for an answer like you or I."

But the *Times* seems positively conventional when compared to the *Financial Times* which is read by an elite in-group with their own esoteric jargon.

Printed on special coloured paper, the journal is virtually indecipherable to the outsider, consisting largely of long lists of numbers which are apparently of mystical significance to the paper's small but dedicated readership.

REVENUE

But just how long can these "way out" papers keep their heads above water ? Most of them find it harder and harder to get advertising and the *Times* relies increasingly on a bizarre "personal" column which has developed into something of a cult. In addition, the refusal of many newsagents to stock the papers means that readers have to rely on unreliable outlets like W H Smith, a provincial firm specialising in erotica and novelties.

"What a country! Even the dogs are going to the dogs."

THE YOUNG IDEA

A FORUM FOR YOUTH IN WHICH RESPONSIBLE MEMBERS OF THE YOUNGER GENERATION TALK FRANKLY AND IDEALISTICALLY ABOUT THEIR BELIEFS

1

Richard Neville-Chamberpot, editor of the new underground paper, *Sinkwithoutatrace*.

Frankly, to my mind, the whole concept, ie, that pot (ie, cannabis resin, as it is known to the fuzz and straights generally) can do you harm, is to my mind wholly ridiculous. Also I think it is completely ridiculous. The latest straight propaganda from some so-called experts who have clearly never turned on, is that pot can damage the human brain and result in damage to brain cells, which makes it hard to speak and think and that. I would like to say that, to my mind, this is a fantastic lie. I have smoked grass for donkey's years, and indeed I have also smoked donkey's ears, but I do not recommend them, as they leave a rather nasty taste in the mouth, something similar to donkey's ears, if you have ever smoked them.

Anyway, were was I ? Oh yes, it is ridiculous to say to my mind that smoking pot results in loss of concentration. By the way, my mate Dave came round on Friday night with this fantastic Burmese stuff, which frankly blew our minds to such an extent that we missed out Saturday and Sunday and didn't come down till Monday night. Anway, as I was trying to say, it is ridiculous to say that smoking joints ever did any harm to anyone, unlike alcohol and drink which is now definitely established by scientists as leading to millions of people getting cancer every year. It is sheer hypocrisy, for instance, for Lord Longford to attack drugs, porn and that, when he is sitting swigging whisky in the House of Lords every night of the week. And as for pot blowing your mind, well, this is quite absurd, I mean, well, frankly, I don't know what they mean, that is, you have only got to look at a copy of our new paper to see the amount of sheer thought which goes into every line of it, I mean we had this story about this H-Bomb they dropped on Wales by mistake, which was totally ignored by the press, except one or two papers like the *Times* and the *Daily Telegraph*, but even then they ignored the vital point which was that the story was not true in the first place. Which reminds me. Dave seems to have gone off with my bird, so I must stop now and then he gave me a book on Black Magic how did he know it was my favourite subject

(discontinued p 94)

2

This week Lady Arabella Churchillcollegecambridge tells why 50 million young people will be in a field near Glastonbury next Tuesday afternoon.

Most people today are totally ignorant of the fact that years ago, long before Mummy and Daddy were born, Glastonbury was one of the seven Mystical Centres in the universe, I mean it was a sort of you know receiving place for messages from all over the galaxy. But you do get this terrific feeling when you're there of this fantastic, well you know it's impossible to explain but most people today have got so many hangups that they can't you know well, get it together. I mean they're too busy earning bread and going on ego-trips.

But the thing is basically that there are these Seven Mystical Centres all over the world in fact all the other six are in

"I'd love to make it with you Brenda, but I don't think it would be worth all the bother."

3

THIS WEEK THE DISTINGUISHED SATIRIST FARTY MELDMAN GIVES HIS FRANK, OUTSPOKEN VIEWS ON THE TOPICAL ISSUE OF OBSCENITY.

Frankly to my mind there is far more obscenity in the Bible than there is in any of the underground press. I mean, take that bit about David murdering Goliath so he could have it off with his wife - that is to my mind the complete nadir of obscenity, but this is read out in churches every Sunday without the fuzz coming in and stopping it.

What most people don't realise, and this is what Richard is trying to say in his classic *Schoolkid's Issue* - of which, by the way, I have a couple of spare copies going, if anyone wants them, at a tenner apiece, but I would be prepared to take a pony for the two. If anyone is interested they should get in touch with Farty Enterprises Ltd, 49-106 Wardour Street, enclosing sae - as I was saying, what Richard is saying basically is that most kids' books are completely without reference to the basic fact of life, ie, sex, and therefore they are obscene, to my way of thinking. You will not find a penis portrayed anywhere in Rupert Bear, Peter Rabbit, Squirrel Nutkin or any of that bourgeois, middle-class rubbish. Also, I mean, *Alice in Wonderland* was written by a kinky clergyman who used to rape hundreds of little girls. That is a well-known historical fact, as anyone who remembers Jonathan Miller's classic film on the TV will remember. This is basically what is really corrupting and should be banned - not photographs of lesbian schoolmistresses masturbating because that is part of life, like all schoolmasters are queer. I mean everyone knows that. It's a psychological fact. I mean, it happened to me. I was coming out of school one night when old Tosser Hargreaves, as we called him, come up to me and suggested (cont p 94)

THE YOUNG IDEA

(continued)

Tibet - have you ever been to Tibet ? Apparently it's absolutely super but no-one's allowed in any more, so there's only Glastonbury left.

Anyway, Andrew Kerr, he used to write Daddy's books for him, he's awfully clever, and he says that if we all meet at Glastonbury on Tuesday afternoon, we can "tap the universe" just like they used to do millions of years ago in the Middle Ages, and all the "earth energy" turned into this fantastic "tree of life" which only blooms on Christmas day, and the Druids realised that so that's what we're doing. *(How much longer must we put up with this kind of rubbish ? Ed).*

Don't get uptight, man, the trouble with you straights is that you're not tuned in to the right vibrations. I mean, one of the things we're going to do is build this fantastic tunnel joining up Glastonbury with Neasden. Did you know that Neasden was originally known as Nugga's Døen which means "The Sacred Centre of the Universe," and originally it was the site of Atlantic which as you know is where the human race

(cont p 94)

Dave Spart, the General Secretary of the National Amalgamated Union of Sixth Form Operatives and Allied Trades, talks frankly and outspokenly about the recent decision of his Union's annual conference, to extend union membership to children at nursery schools, playgroups and kindergartens.

Basically, to my mind, more and more people are coming round to the view, ie, that is that children in the 1 - 6 age bracket are basically more exploited than any other age-bracket. Just imagine it for a moment. From morning to night, these kids are pushed about. Nappies are pinned on them, regardless of their wishes. They are force-fed via bottles and forced into eating at all hours of day and night without consultation and without any form of meaningful dialogue taking place. In fact they have no say in dictating their environment whatsoever. Basically this is an affront to human dignity. We have therefore laid down the following guidelines with regard to giving a basic statement of what constitute the rights of infants apropos their domestic environment and conditions of work, viz:

1. That all infants have the right to determine their timetable. There should be preliminary consultations with representatives of parental management with regard to all living conditions, eg, getting up, going to bed and having baths, which are frequently employed by parental management as disorientation techniques.

2. Thirdly, private toilet facilities should be made freely available without discrimination and regardless of race or colour. Our researches show that in 86 per cent of cases infants are subjected to humiliation by being forced to perform toilet movement in a public environment. It is a well-known fact that these techniques were used in Nazi concentration camps (cont p 94)

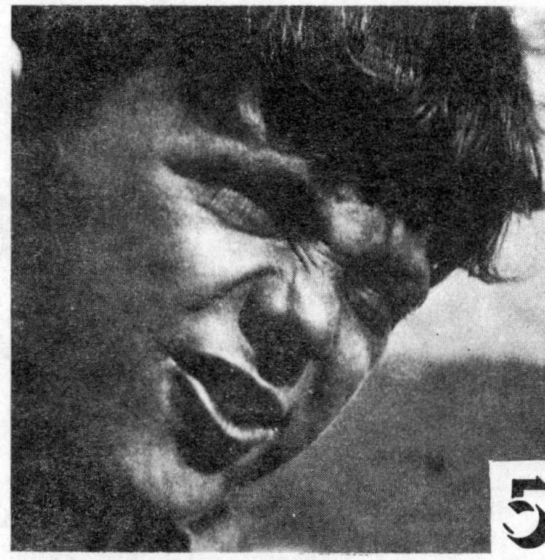

"Our aim is the total overthrow of bourgeois capitalism as we know it today. We are witnessing the birth-pangs of a totally new concept in the restructuralisation of post-capitalist society, in which the old patterns of restrictivist and monopolistic ownership-control are disintegrating under the pressures of their inherent contradiction within the class system, in itself a meaningless concept, and as Marx has demonstrated, the past is behind us and we have only the future to look forward to, man."

So speaks one of the most articulate and militant members of the outstanding new generation of revolutionaries who, all over Britain, are giving the biggest impetus to the politics of the extreme left since the heady days of the Spanish war.

He is Ron Thribb, 17, chairman of the Hull Polytechnic League of International Anarcho-Syndicalists. Although his group at present has only seven members, it is expanding fast and is attracting attention from as far away as Grimsby and Scunthorpe.

Not everyone at Hull agrees, however, with Thribb's tactics for the overthrow of the capitalist system. One such is Raymond Thribb, Ron's 16-year-old brother, who says: "Basically, man" (cont p 94)

A STEP forward in the right direction in the English legal system was taken last Monday when the Family Division of the High Court sat for the first time.

Financial Times

ETERNAL YOUTH

for only 10 min's simple exercise

For millions of years the Holy Men of India (or Gnomins, as they are known) have practised the mystical art of GNOGA. It is their way of achieving total relaxation, a sense of complete well-being and an active married life which can last well into old age.

GNOGA consists of a set of progressively simple excercises involving all parts of the human body.

But they are unlike any kind of exercise you've ever come across before!

To the Indian, the idea of doing press-ups and going for long runs, followed by cold baths, would seem barbaric. Instead the Gnomins practise what they call *Sleepin*.

This involves placing the body in a horizontal position, preferably on some soft, springy surface and allowing the limbs to assume a state of complete relaxation.

A WARNING

All this may sound straightforward enough. But GNOGA experts, with their millions of years of experience, are insistent that unless performed under EXPERT GUIDANCE the exercise of GNOGA can lead to severe physical and brain damage, and in some cases even a terminal experience (or "Dheath" as it is known to the Holy Men of the East).

That is why it is vital that, before you set off on the Mystical 73-fold path to Eternal Youth, you fill in the form below to become officially enrolled as a bona fide student in the GNOGA Institute of Advanced Relaxation.

ONE MORE THING

As you advance along the path of Gnogic Ecstasy, you will come to realise that mere physical excercises are only the first step towards Total Bliss. Eventually the Gnogic Path will mean a complete change in your way of life. Among other things this will involve a renunciation of many aspects of our materialistic Western way of life. Above all, you will come to see that the greatest obstacle to a state of complete GNOGANA is the possession of money. It is then that our highly-trained experts will visit your home to advise you on the ancient GNOGA method of divesting yourself of all your monetary assets. Only when this final obstacle has been surmounted, will you be left alone in a state of complete peace and relaxation to enjoy Gnogana in the privacy of your own home (or Salvation Army hostel, as the ancients have known it for millions of years).

On receipt of your application, we shall send you a FREE brochure giving full details of some of the thousands of ways in which we can help you achieve a state of advanced bliss, or GNOGANA as it is known to mystics the world over.

Here are just some of the thousands of ways in which the Gnoga Institute of Advanced Relaxation will be able to help you to obtain the Secret of Eternal Youth.

1.

1. Fully-illustrated 1000-page book *The Wit and Wisdom of the East* by Sir Rabindranath Worsthorne OBE, bound in hand-tooled Gnomitex with embossed gold spine. Normal price £75. Special offer 25p.

CAN BE YOURS

a day!!

2.

2. A set of eight 12" Long Playing gramophone records of Music of the Orient played by world-famous Oriental musician and Gnoga-expert Yhudi Menonly, and Swami Mantovani's Benares Strings, conducted by Lord Clark of Civvy Street, Amritsar.

3.

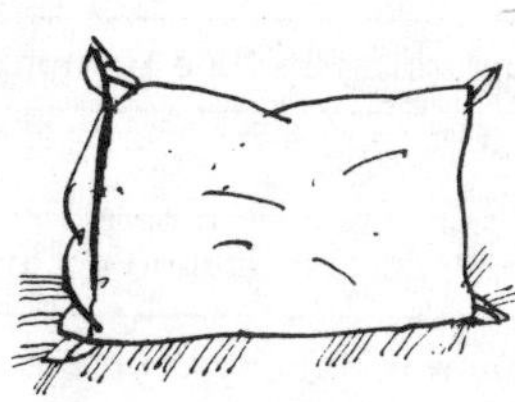

3. Herbal Feather Pillow, woven from genuine Kashmir-style Tomalin, of the type used by Gnomins for millions of years to induce profound relaxation for anything up to eight hours a night.

4.

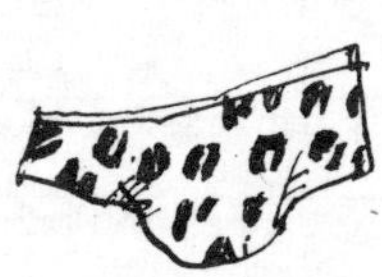

4. See-through leopard-skin-style LOINCLOTH, of the type popularised on TV by world-famous Fakir Mahatma Muggerishi.

5.

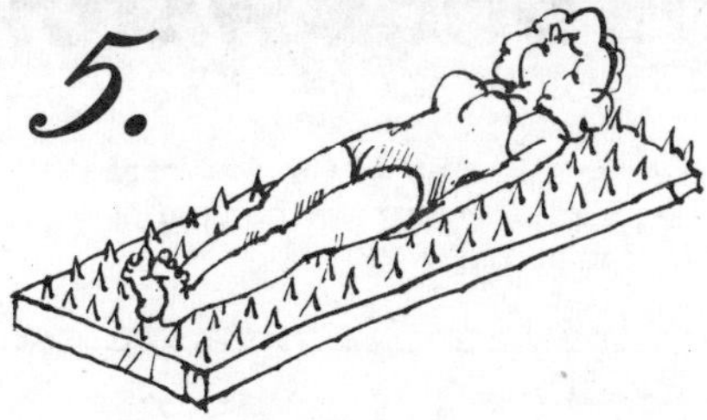

5. An absolute MUST for all would-be GNOMINS - Bed of Nails, made with softee-spunge latex that look JUST LIKE THE REAL THING. Amaze your friends as you lie down in your see-through leopard-skin-style Loincloth, of the type publicised on TV by world-famous Fakir Mahatma Muggerishi, without apparently experiencing any pain!

FREE GIFT & EXAMINATION CERTIFICATE

Please rush me all the above and I promise to pay the ridiculously low figure of £297.47 on delivery, plus 12 monthly instalments of £215.

Name.........................

Address......................

....

....

Cheques payable to Karsh and Curry Ltd (Photographs and Oriental Foods), Gnome House, Neasdelhi, India.

POLLUTION CORNER

YOUR DOOMWATCH GUIDE

TO WHAT THEY'RE ALL ON ABOUT

Yes, they're all on about the new craze that's sweeping the country - the coming extinction of mankind!

Here's your easy to learn, at-a-glance guide to what it all means, your very own cut-out-and-keep Dictionary for Doomsday.

DOOMWATCH	- A programme that used to be on the telly.
ENVIRONMENT	- Ecosystem
ECOSYSTEM	- (see Environment)
ENVIRONMENTALIST	- A man with a beard on television
ECOLOGIST	- See Environmentalist
DOOMWATCH	- A lot of old tins on a beach
EXPONENTIAL	- Something going up (see Unemployment)
POLLUTION	- The exhaust fumes from someone else's car
NATURAL CYCLES	- What everyone else should go to work on
ENVIRONMENTAL CRISIS	- A lot of men with beards on the telly
ECOLOGIST	- A magazine
NATURE	- Another magazine
SCIENTIFIC WASTE MANAGEMENT CONSULTANTS	- Dustmen
DE-URBANISATION	- Going to the country
RESOURCE-USING AND POLLUTING TECHNOLOGIES	- Cars
SPACESHIP EARTH	- A silly expression taken up by the Observer
OPERATION DOOMWATCH	- A silly expression taken up by the Sun, Daily Mirror, etc.
ECOLOGICAL IMBALANCE	- A lot of old tins in my garden instead of the next one
BIOSPHERE	- See Ecosystem
TECHNOSPHERE	- See Doomwatch
SPHERE	- Another magazine (now defunct)

The 'Switch off - turn in - drop off' drug that is paralysing Britain

Tonight in all parts of Britain millions of men, women and even children will surrender themselves to the hypnotic influence of one of the most powerful and sinister drugs known to man *(writes Lunchtime O'Booze)*.

The drug is known as SLEEP. Sleep has been known about for millions of years - but it is only recently that scientists working round the clock have woken up to its full menacing potential.

Killer

What happens to someone who succumbs to this drug's deceptive influence ?

Within a few minutes, say the scientists, his eyes will glaze and close. His speech becomes slurred and he eventually loses the capacity of speech altogether.

As the full effects of the drug take hold, the addict slumps down in a state of semi-paralysis.

Here he may remain for anything up to ten or more hours.

Good Heavens

Why do they do it ? One addict who prefers to remain anonymous says: "It is just fantastic. You're taken right out of your mind. On a good 'kip' you can see the most fantastic visions. Sometimes you feel you're flying. You see these fantastic colours - and another great thing is that there are no after effects. In fact you often feel better than when you started, or 'turned in' as we 'kippies' call it."

ZZZZZZ

Already a whole sub-culture has sprung up around the "sleeping kick." The users employ a whole variety of slang terms to describe their drug - "having a doze", or a "snooze," "taking a nap", "forty winks," "hitting the hay," "dossing down," or "getting the head down for an hour or two before breakfast."

Many addicts even put aside a special room in their houses to practise their "sleeping" activities. And in recent years, millions of people, particularly young teenagers and newly-weds, have taken to doing it together.

Nevertheless, for all the claims that "sleeping" is harmless, growing fears are being expressed by scientists and others about the long-term effects of the drug.

There seems little doubt that a large proportion of driving accidents are caused by motorists "nodding off" at the wheel.

Scientists are beginning to suggest that every year no less than millions of people may actually be dying while under the influence of "sleep."

More serious still, recent figures confirm that several hundred million man-hours are lost to British industry every day through the growth of the "sleep habit" - costing the country the equivalent of anything up to 5,913,640 Concordes in a full year.

Bed Shocks

A group of influential Sir Gerald Nabarro's, led by a Tory backbencher, are lobbying the government to introduce legislation that would compel the manufacturers of pyjamas, blankets and nightcaps to print on their product the warning "Sleep is Dangerous to the Economy."

"Another poison pen letter!"

FFOLKES

"Tomorrow will be in the low seventies with scattered showers."

TV with PETER BLACKOUT

TINY TONY

Millions wept openly last night at the showing of the documentary *Watch the Birdie!*, a deeply moving account of the everyday life of "a royal photographer of restricted growth." (The expression "Lord Snowdon," we were told, is no longer used, as being likely to cause offence).

Few of us can ever know what it is like to be "a royal photographer of restricted growth," but certainly after last night few of us can ever look at him again without a deep sense of compassion.

Princess Midget

"What you have to live with" said the "royal photographer of restricted growth," "is constantly being stared at in the street and ridiculed. People somehow think of one as some kind of a freak, or connected with the circus."

"Mind you, not all 'royal photographers of restricted growth' (the expression 'Lord Snowdon' is no longer used as being offensive) have had the luck, as I have, to find a sympathetic employer in the shape of Lord Thomson. He is fully aware of my disabilities but fortunately he has been prepared to overlook them in view of the fact that I am 'a royal photographer of restricted growth.' "

Royal Flash

"I have been also extremely fortunate, unlike many 'royal photographers of restricted growth,' in finding someone suffering from the same disability as myself, although she is not herself a photographer. Mind you," he quipped with a boyish grin, "she makes a pretty picture."

The film ended with a poignant scene showing ' the royal photographer of restricted growth' sitting alone in his enormous Palace, exposing his negatives in the privacy of his darkroom.

We are left with the abiding impression of a man who, for all our compassion and sympathy, is doomed to the solitary and miserable life of 'a royal photographer of restricted growth.'

Market CORNER

EVERY WEEK FROM NOW UNTIL 1977, A TEAM OF EXPERTS IN EVERY FIELD WILL BE ON CALL TO ANSWER YOUR QUERIES AS TO WHAT LIFE WILL BE LIKE WHEN BRITAIN BECOMES A MEMBER OF THE EUROPEAN ECONOMIC COMMUNITY.

THIS WEEK YOUR RESIDENT EXPERT IS THE ECONOMIST WILLIAM DAVIS.

Q. Many foreigners are unkind to animals. We have a baby swan. Will it be safe or will Spanish peasants kick it in the street ? *(Mrs B F, Ongar)*.

A. I can't say where they'll kick it, madam. But your swan certainly won't like it!!

Q. Are you trying to be funny ? *(E.E.C. Brussels)*.

A. No. I'm just trying.

Q. Assuming the basic instability of the fluctuation in consumer durables, what is the medium term outlook with regard to the predicted slump in the investment cycle give or take a non-variable surplus over and above that predicted by the International Economic & Fiscal Bureau of Statistics ? *(P J, Ealing)*.

A. I thought you'd never ask!!! But seriously, folks, it's easier than it sounds. If the upturn in total currency reserves equals or exceeds the margin of "invisible" increase in sterling assets, then we should confidently expect an interim imbalance which would stabilize productivity factors on an across the board basis with an equivalent increase in consumer activity, not withstanding the bi-ennial destocking in market liabilities.

That Six

You ask

This week, our resident expert is Professor Hugh Trevor-Europa.

Q: Will our stamps still have the Queen's head on ? *(Mrs E R London, SW 1).*

A: *Of course, they will, you silly old bag.*

Q: When we get into Europe, does it mean that alien folk of every hue will be swarming into our already overcrowded hospitals ? *(Mr E P, Wolverhampton).*

A: *Come off it, grandad, we're not living in the Middle Ages, and, like it or not, we've got to move with the times.*

Q: Given the proposed modifications in the infrastructure of the agricultural support system, is it not likely the cost-viability per production unit at the secondary level of non-exportables will rise pro rata with the advance costing of the productivity schedules? *(Prof. N.K, Cambridge).*

A: *Gor blimey, Einstein, you nearly had us stumped there! But the answer is, of course, no. The invisible assets which will accrue from the new infrastructure should more than counteract any drain on the bilateral balances of the post-inflationary wage-price-cost-productivity spiral. So now you know. Got it ?*

Q: Is it true that all the newspapers will be written in a foreign language ? *(L C of C, Kent).*

A: *Nein. Es non vero. Tutti il dagblatten vil be scribe en ein lingua communale, comme this, mate!*

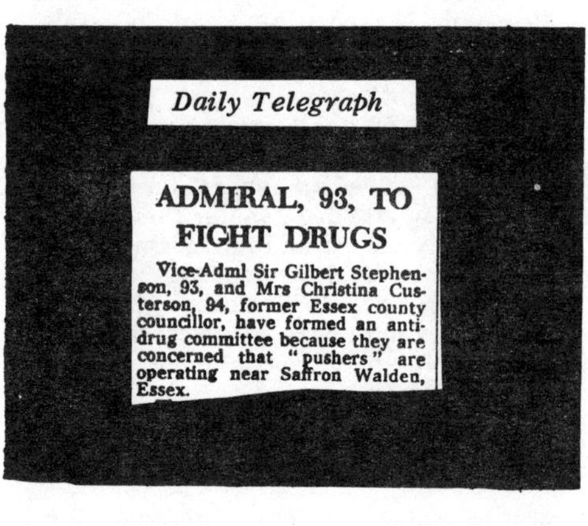

Daily Telegraph

ADMIRAL, 93, TO FIGHT DRUGS

Vice-Adml Sir Gilbert Stephenson, 93, and Mrs Christina Custerson, 94, former Essex county councillor, have formed an anti-drug committee because they are concerned that "pushers" are operating near Saffron Walden, Essex.

AT THE THEATRE

ANYONE FOR MENACE?

by
Ronald Bryden-Pier

Harold Pinter's new play *Hard Up* is an enigma without a variation, a riddle without a sphinx. It is, as we might expect, an exquisitely scored study in ambivalence, etched in the sombre tones of a Hokusai miniature. The theme, for it can hardly be described as an Etrucan vase, centres round the figure of a middle-aged playwright, sitting alone in a darkened room, wracking his brain for a subject for his new play. All he knows is that there must be a part for his actress wife, a leggy, electric, menacing, high-heeled, silk-stockinged actress, who likes nothing better than to play leggy, electric, menacing, high-heeled, silk-stockinged actresses in plays about leggy, electric *(Stop this and get on with the story. Ed.)*

Well, there isn't much of a story actually. It seems from the few stray remarks that he utters in between lighting cigarettes, watching television and staring moodily at the ceiling, that the playwright is very successful. Some years before, he had been singled out by the critics as an entirely new sort of playwright, specialising in 'creating an atmosphere of hidden menace out of nothing at all'. In fact, the playwright knows that he has succeeded in hoodwinking the public with his dramatic sleight-of-hand. By now, after a number of highly-paid Hollywood film scripts, he is comfortably off and lives in a luxurious Regents Park flat, surrounded by erotic pictures. But what can he do, except go on writing the same old meaningless rubbish?

In fact, as we gather from his maundering conversation, he is living increasingly in the past. Occasionally he breaks into snatches of Edwardian music hall songs, or remarks to his wife that he is looking forward to the Second World War. But more frequently, he is lost in a nostalgic reverie for the gay times they had together when they were young.

"Do you remember that restaurant we used to go to?" he asks at one point. "Do you remember that old Trevor Howard film, what was it called?" he enquires at another. "Do you remember my next line?" his wife suddenly asks, "we haven't got a prompter." "Yes we have!" comes back a faint squeaky voice from the wings. It is the most dramatic moment of the play, and it is followed by one of those prolonged Pinteresque silences, pregnant with unspoken terror. After several minutes, the lights go up, and we are at once transported into a quite different world - a large well-lit room, full of middle-aged playgoers battling at a counter for small glasses of warm gin, and saying to each other in loud middle-class voices: "Isn't it marvellous the way he manages to conjure up an atmosphere of hidden menace out of nothing at all?"

The interval, for that is what it is, lasts for two hours. and thus becomes, by a brilliant *coup de theatre,* the central and most meaningful part of the play. This is pure Pinter, at its most imaginative and macabre. I implore you all to go and see it. This one will run and run. A show for all the family. (Please put up outside theatre, and send you-know-what to you-know-where.)

Dear Bryden-Pier,

It is now some five years since you took over as our Dramatic Critic. I have keenly admired all that you have done for the paper during this period, but I am beginning to wonder whether you would appreciate a sabbatical decade, which you have well earned. Unfortunately, owing to circumstances which you will no doubt understand, we shall be unable to continue your salary during this period, but feel certain you will welcome this opportunity to look for another job.

Yours sincerely,
THE EDITOR

P.S. I am sure you will appreciate the 'hidden menace' in this letter! (Just my little joke!)

"I'll be glad when there's just One Nation. I never did like the other one."

Angry Brigade

YARD SWOOPS

by Our Crime Correspondent

A remote Somerset mansion was last night the scene of a massive one-man swoop by bleary-eyed but triumphant Inspector "Knacker of the Yard" Knacker.

The swoop brought an end to the months-long campaign of terror waged by the group calling themselves "the Angry Brigade."

ANARCHY

Two men who were helping police with their enquiries late last night at Midsummer Nightsdream Police Station were W. Rees-Mogg, 41, described as a journalist, and L. Thomson of Fleet, 107, a company director.

Police had been drawn to the house, the home of Mogg, by the fact that the only concrete evidence of the "Angry Brigade's" existence was a series of notes delivered at regular intervals to the offices of *The* Times, a small-circulation newspaper published in London, of which Mogg is the editor.

ANGRY BRIGADIER HAMILTON

The notes followed in each case "bomb incidents" at the homes of prominent public figures.

But the suspicions of the police were aroused by the fact that no-one was even hurt in the explosions, and moreover that in each case *The Times* gained a good deal of publicity from the reprinting of the "notes" alleged to have been received from members of the gang.

STUNT

Last night Insp. Knacker told reporters: "It was clear to me from the word go that this was nothing more nor less than a crude publicity campaign organised by a paper trying desperately to keep its head above water."

Insp. Knacker is 49.

Daily Telegraph

COMPUTER TO REVISE PRAYERS

By Dr CECIL NORTHCOTT Churches Correspondent

A COMPUTER has been used to speed up revision of the Church of England Prayer Book.

The Anglican Liturgical Commission has fed hundreds of criticisms and suggestions on experimental services into a computer for analysis and classification as part of the preparation for the revision.

OUR ECCLESIASTICAL CORRESPONDENT THE REV. "JUMBO" JETTE WRITES:

I understand that Church leaders are "delighted" with the first fruits of the labours of CRANMER (Computerised Rationalisation And New-Style Modernisation of Ecclesiastical Ritual), as the 400-year-old computer housed at Lambeth Palace is known to the team of

MY NEW LOVE

by Our Showbiz Correspondent BOGUS CASHIN (no relation)

Top TV Comic Larry Laughs who spr to fame as compere of 'Monday night at t Neasden Hippodrome' way back in the 50 announced his plans to marry future teen beauty queen Euphorbia Clint, 16, last n

Miss Clint, 13, rose to fame on Mr La knees on his recent TV series *'Guess My Weight'* in which contestants from all ove the country sat on Mr Laughs' knees and tried to guess his weight.

Nasty

"It was not love at first sight" said Mis Clint last night. "It was more a gradual growing warmth between us."

But what about the age-gap?, I asked M Laughs. With that twinkling grin that has market researchers working on the project.

One of the first passages to be "fed in" to CRANMER was the so-called Lord's Prayer, now renamed "Memo To Head Office". This now runs as follows:

TO WHOM IT MAY CONCERN

Dear Sir or Madam (at above address),

Your name has been personally selected by our computer out of thousands living in your area. Your instructions are receiving our careful attention, at all levels. We trust that you will continue to meet our day-to-day requirements as they may arise. We apologise for any inconvenience caused, and trust that this feeling will be mutual. We hope that you will be good enough not to place any demands more than strictly necessary on our already overstretched resources. We trust that we can both avoid unpleasantness in this matter.

Assuring you of our best attention and highest esteem at all times.

Yours sincerely,

Our ref: 23b4721Xz02
Wedgebenn Patents Pending

"In a moment, my child, we'll see what the computer comes up with in the way of penance."

'She's 15' by Top TV Comic 78

him a household name in denture-manufacturing circles, he said :" You're as young as you feel."

He then fell to the floor, giving his famous Dead-Man-Lying-On-The-Floor routine which has brought chuckles to a million homes.

Revolting

"It's a laugh-a-minute with Larry", said pretty 12 year-old dancer Euphorbia Clint last night. "He's a proper gent of the old school. I do not mind him being old. Larry has taught me a lot about life.

"I tell you, when I saw him for the first time being wheeled onto the stage with his world-famous catch phrase: "Give us a push, someone" I frankly thought to myself, 'What a silly old bugger. I wonder what people see in him.' But then came the moment when I sat on his knee and I realised there was more to him than meets the eye."

At her North Poplar home last night Mrs Laughs, who was married to Larry for 40 years, said: "She's welcome to the old fart frankly. It will be a great weight off my shoulders." Mr Laughs is 193.

"Sprinkle some Biognome on your garden and see the difference"

says Harry Gnomecroft

No more digging! No more weeding! Cut out all that back-breaking work! Now at last sit back and let this amazing new Garden miracle get to work amongst your plants.

"Biognome is the gardening discovery of the century" says world-famous moustachioed bore Harry Gnomecroft. "It contains incredible new ingredients hitherto unknown to scientists which have the power to transform a barren patch of earth into a colourful paradise pulsating with life."

So says frightful old hairychops Gnomecroft, whose green fingers can turn barren old pennies into glittering pound notes overnight.

Just sprinkle a three ton sack of Biognome on your garden and watch as within minutes all weeds disappear as IF BY MAGIC.

Then — thrill with amazement as your lifeless pansies thrust through the soil like something out of a fairy tale and are transformed into six-foot high prize-winning blooms.

Get the shock of your life, says bewhiskered gaffer-style old fool Gnomecroft, as your roses take off like Boeing-style jets and engulf your house with lavish evergreen foliage and giant-size flowers as big as footballs.

No digging. No raking. Just fork out £512 for a 2oz jumbo-style sachet of BIOGNOME. Sprinkle it on the vegetable patch and have CARROTS well over three feet long; KING SIZE radishes as big as melons; succulent juicy gooseberries as long as rhubarb; ENORMOUS monster-style peas bursting out of their pods like bullets and hitting you on the nose while you are sitting in your deck chair watching the miracle substance going about its astonishing business.

And what about drought? Says red-faced handlebarred entrepreneur Gnomecroft: "There is enough natural moisture in one grain of my Biognome to keep your plants fully watered three hundred and sixty five days of the year."

Throw your mower on the scrap-heap and turn your lawn into an ever-verdant carpet of soft velvet, says ridiculous buffoon Gnomecroft.

Biognome contains a revolutionary ingredient, hitherto unknown to science, which actually CUTS your grass as it grows. This ingredient simultaneously repels all slugs, moles and birds with tiny scientific "bullets" invisible to the naked eye and COMPLETELY harmless to domestic animals and human beings.

AT LAST an end to unwanted stones brick and rubble! When Biognome goes to work, says hirsute twit Gnomecroft, it transforms all these obstacles into crumbly rich high-protein humus, the type that all plants thrive on.

Write now for the wonder sample that will change your garden into a Heaven on Earth.

To: Gnome Garden Products Ltd, Floral House, 86/109 Commercial Road, City Centre, Neasden-on-Trent, Staffs.
Name ....
Address ....

Walter Blezard

Levin it up

By the by, I have spent an anxious moment or two since the death last October of M. Alphonse Enorme, the patron of the Petit Jardin des Pooves in Nevers-sur-Dimanche, nestling as it does in the thickly-carpeted heart of the Cadillac country. With the departure of M. Enorme the world can never be the same again and I will certainly never be the same again for it was in the little vine-trellised patio of M. Enorme's five-star hostelry that I consumed what were without the faintest shadow of a doubt some of the most delicious mouth-watering spoonfuls of Brown Windsor soup that have ever flowed through my gullet and down into the ample vaults of my stomach, and I speak as one into the ample vaults of whose stomach a considerable number of spoonfuls of Brown Windsor soup have flowed at one time or another in my long and if I may say so eventful career as a sampler of the many different varieties of the rich, thick, dark liquid substance that is known throughout the world - and if there is another world beyond I see no reason why the same nomenclature should not apply - as Brown Windsor soup.

It was here (needless to say) that I first set eyes on Mr Bernard Levin, a small diminutive gentleman whose youthful, nay schoolboyish appearance belied his 43 years. Surely there was never such a one as this Levin, a man of whom it was said by no less a person than one of his many contemporaries (whose name incidentally escapes me, though, to be sure, it was on the tip of my tongue only a second ago) that there was never such a one as he - and personally I see no good reason - nor (for that matter) any bad reason for disassociating myself from that verdict, though, indeed, however curious it may seem to some, there will always be those who, for reasons best known to themselves will do so (though what it is they will do I frankly have no idea - since this sentence began a long , long time ago and for the life of me I cannot recall how the matter arose in the first place, if indeed it did ever arise, and doubtless there will be those who will say that it did, and there will equally be those who will say that it did not, but I will not take sides in any such dispute for, as I have already made clear I have forgotten if indeed I ever knew what it was that I was talking about in the first place.

What an amazing little fellow he was to be sure! One day he would produce as fine a piece of invective as one could ever hope to see printed in the pages of *The Times* - it could be an attack on Lord Rothermere or a brilliantly executed portrait in vitriol of the late Lord Goddard - in either event his sharp and piercing barbs were sufficient to draw blood - whether it was in the shape of a High Court writ, in the case of the aforementioned newspaper proprietor - or in the latter instance, a High Court rant emanating from the person of the Master of the Rolls himself.

But then, mark the change, when the next day or week or month, it matters not which, Mr Levin's barbs would be carefully put to one side and another character quite, quite different would emerge - a second-rate sentimental pedlar of shmaltz - rhapsodising in the worst possible taste on the music of Wagner (or the paintings of Durer) - or, for that matter the Brown Windsor soup of the type obtainable at the Petit Jardin des Pooves in Nevers-sur-Dimanche nestling as it does in the thickly carpeted heart of (cont p 94)

Neasden fans in bomb threat scare shock

by E. I. Addio

Our Man In the Shower Room with the Wandering Fingers

Neasden fans last night threatened to bomb the headquarters of the Football Association following the F A's decision to shut down the Neasden Bridge Stadium for an indefinite period.

The ban came as the result of the widespread rioting and outbreaks of guerilla warfare during the final of the North Circular Relegation Trophy v. Dollis Hill.

THIN RED LINESMAN

The trouble began when thin red linesman seven-stone weakling, Wally Engels, 73, self-styled Chairman of the 1-man Neasden Soviet For Universal Peace, flagged Neasden and Scotland International "Wee Jimmy Porridge following an alleged assault on the Dollis Hill goalie during the "warm up" period prior to kick-off.

Neasden fans, Sid and Doris Bonkers, swarmed onto the pitch and attacked the referee, the late Sid Himmler, before setting fire to the directors' box.

SHOCK

Last night, tight-lipped manager, Ron Knee, 59, condemned the F A's decision from his holiday chalet in Neasdemelinos, Spain.

Looking bronzed and fat, an ashed-faced Knee told reporters:

"This is highly irregular to my mind to single out one club to pay the price for all the violence in the world.

"We provide great entertainment at Neasden Bridge. Just because a few fans burn down the studium just for a bit of insurance money - woops - I mean, to register their sincerely-felt protest against the indifferent refereeing that we suffer through lack of a professional body with full authoritative powers to control the game from the middle."

Asked to complete his sentence, Knee snapped:

"It had gone on far too long. It was high time it came to an end."

Mr Knee is 59.

LATE SCORE

INTER-SUBURBS EUROPEAN CUP (Replay)

F C Omo (Delft) 10 Neasden 0

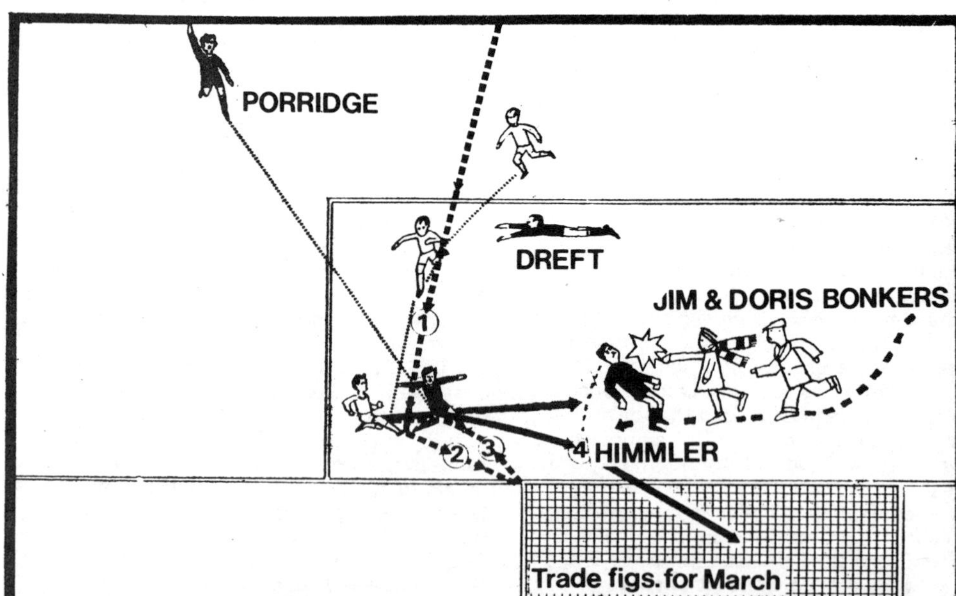

"I've fought the church for years to have squash racquets included in Exorcism Kits!"

"Er . . . . mind if we swear?"

Pay as you enter

Some people aren't helpful at all. That's what London Transport thinks, anyway.

Some people still haven't noticed that when they get onto one of the new London buses they need to have the right change.

It's such a simple matter, really. You only need a couple of twopenny pieces (no 1p pieces, please! Our machines don't like them!)

You'd think most people would have caught on by now, wouldn't you ?

But they haven't, the stupid idiots.

That's why we have to pay for expensive full-page advertisements like this.

And that means the fares have to go up again, doesn't it ?

Just because silly, thoughtless, selfish people like you haven't got the nous to learn the ropes of hopping on a 'bus Seventies-style.

Just look at you. You get on a bus, blithely expecting that you can ask the driver to change your money for you.

Who do you think we are ? A Bank ?

And while you're standing there looking pathetic, fumbling for the right coins, don't you realise that you're holding up everybody else.

Can you wonder that all our carefully scheduled services get behind, when there are people like you throwing spanners in the works ?

Is it surprising that fleets of No 11's pile up one behind another ? Or that bus-drivers have to "crawl" for miles, creating huge traffic jams ?

Is it surprising that London's entire traffic system is grinding to a halt, and that rush-hour commuters are herded to and from their work like robots - when there are stupid morons like you around who can't be bothered to see that they've got the right change in their pockets before they leave home in the morning.

So isn't it time you pulled yourself together, you appalling little twit ?

We're doing *our* best.

Our machines are doing *their* best.

It's only YOU who's letting the side down.

No wonder life in London these days is becoming intolerable. No wonder that everyone is so irritable and rude. No wonder that our mental hospitals are jammed packed to overflowing. No wonder that ordinary people like London Transport, trying to do their best, are getting blamed for almost every little thing that goes wrong nowadays.

It's all YOUR FAULT

(Issued by the Department of the Environment and London Transport in aid of International Friendship Year and the World Wild Life Fund).

OBSERVER REVIEW

THE PRIVATE LIFE OF VIRGINIA WOOLF-1

UNDER THE SHADOW OF MADNESS

For many years Rogèr Launcelot Bell was a second cousin of the late Duncan Woolf, the painter and decorator who was related by marriage to Vanessa St. Loe Grant, a lifelong friend of Madge Atkins, Lytton Strachey's masseuse. She first met Lawrence Lamb at Cornelia Garnett's famous Private View at the Carrington Gallery in 1928. Later she was to form the basis of the character of Miss Dooders in Virginia Woolf's novel Carry on up the Lighthouse, and was a regular guest at the famous Tuesday afternoon Bathing Parties at the Bloomsbury Essoldo. It was not until 1936 that she became a cousin of Leonard Brezhnev, the poet and signwriter whose brother Gustav Mahler "did" for Virginia Woolf before committing suicide at the tragically early age of 91. Here, in an extract from her forthcoming book 'Just a Fawn at Twilight' (the fourth volume of her trilogy 'Hello Sailor') she reveals hitherto unknown facts about the enigma of Clive Strachey's trip to Clacton in 1912.

Lytton Strachey's appearance was truly remarkable, and has been vividly described by Clive Clive in his privately printed memoir *Reduced To Clear:*

"Lytton Strachey's appearance was truly remarkable. He reminded one at first sight of one of Gaudier Blavatsky's sleeping postmen at the height of his Blue Period. At second sight he resembled more a startled marmoset, viewing the world anxiously through his enormous brown eyes, so vividly captured in Henry Moore's equestrian statue of him, which has now been incorporated into the Basildon New Town Butch Cassidy Shopping Precinct."

Virginia Woolf's appearance has been best caught perhaps by Angelico Mullard's famous photograph, now in the possession of Duncan Garsington, himself a close friend of Ron Hall, whose house at Dollis Hill became the meeting place of The Bores, the Cambridge Society which included Rupert Strange, Bertrand Pevsner, E.G. Keynes, W.F. Sibley and Mary Kenny. Lord David Woolf, in a vivid phrase, described her as looking "like an old sheep that had been struck by lightning".

One fact that has never been commented on was the fact that neither of them, either Lytton Strachey or Virginia Woolf, was ever seen together.

This phenomenon haunted me for many years and prompted me to undertake investigations which ended in a truly remarkable discovery one hot afternoon at *The Old Mill By The Stream*, the caravan rented by Lytton and Carrington from the late Lady Godiva Clark (no relation).

Lytton had been particularly brilliant during tea. He had a strong streak of malice, and he was throwing off explosive epigrams that flashed and glittered like firecrackers, none of which I can now remember. All his observations, however, were at the expense of poor Virginia herself. Suddenly, to my utter surprise, his beard fell off. I looked again, and could hardly believe the evidence of my own eyes. It was Virginia.

Now I understood it all: the high squeaky voice, his ill-concealed fondness for other men, his pale, wandering hands.

Snatching a heavy Luger from her handbag, Lytton pointed it at me with her eyes glinting madly.

"Squeal, Buster, and I'll blow your pesky head off!" she rasped, in the unmistakeable Stracheyan tone that we had come to know so well, and seizing a woollen tea-cosy, she drew it furtively over her head and minced away into the house.

She reappeared a moment later, her beard glued firmly back into place, and looking exactly as if nothing had happened.

NEXT WEEK: Lord Goodman intervenes: Virginia's fondness for other women explained.

"I'm either drinking too much or the dawn comes up like thunder."

LUXURY HOTEL 'WORSE THAN AUSCHWITZ'

say holiday couple

by Lunchtime O'Booze

A Neasden couple, Mr and Mrs Reggie Lenin, were the centre of a storm that threatened to rock Britain's booming holiday industry to its foundations yesterday.

Mr and Mrs Lenin were met by reporters at Gatwick Airport, after spending only two days of their 14-day, all-inclusive £194.86p luxury "superholiday" at the new Greek island of Nesdos.

Said Lenin, 46, of Pardine Avenue, Neasden: "It was hell on earth. I have seen nothing like it since we had the Blitz on *All Our Yesterdays*"

Horror

Mr Lenin described how he and his blonde wife, Antonia, booked the holiday from a Gnomitours colour brochure in January 1957.

"We have been saving up all our lives for this holiday of a lifetime" chipped in a tearful Mrs Lenin.

"In the photo it looked an idyllic spot. There was this great big hotel with white towers and a beautiful swimming pool in front."

Last night a Gnomitours spokesman said: "It seems there has been some misunderstanding. The picture of the Taj Mahal only appeared on some of the brochures. Luckily the mistake was spotted after only 5,000,000 copies had been printed."

Squalor

Mr Lenin described what actually happened when they reached the so-called island of Nesdos.

"It wasn't even built yet" he said. "The workmen were still pouring the cement into the sea. We spent the night on board the ship which was bringing the sand for the beach."

Added shapely Mrs Lenin: "It was worse than Auschwitz. They said in the brochure the hotel was only 'ten minutes walk from the beach' but there wasn't even a beach, let alone a hotel. All I got for my holiday was mosquito bites, and I could get those anytime, 4p off in the Neasdimart, Hurry, Hurry, Hurry while stocks last."

Amazing

"It is quite true the Nesdos development has run into a few snags in recent months" admitted a spokesman for Gnomitours last night, "but we are doing everything we can to get the island finished as soon as possible.

"Unfortunately we are not in a position to refund any of the moneys subscribed by our clients, owing to the fact that they have already been indented for on our computer. However, we have filled out the sun-roof of the Gnomitour offices in Neasden High Street with deck-chairs, beach umbrellas etc, and we are making these facilities freely available to our clients at only a token additional charge of £57."

Neasden man wins Nobel Prize

by our Neasden Affairs Correspondent

A 57-year-old Neasden man, Mr Solly Neasden (pronounced Solyznitzysn) has been awarded the Nobel Prize for services to Literature.

The announcement was made yesterday and it is bound to cause a storm of considerable proportions in Neasden.

HERO

Mr Solly Neasden who has been compared by some critics to such literary giants as Godfrey Winn and George G. Ale, has written many works which are highly critical of life in Neasden.

His most famous work "One Day in the Life of Arthur Sprarg" presents a dismal picture of the dreariness of Neasden life as seen through the eyes of a municipal laundromat supervisor.

GIANT

But despite his critical approach Mr Neasden has many times stated his devotion to "Mother Neasden." In 1968 he told reporters: "I have lived my life here. Neasden means everything to me. I could never leave."

But it remains a matter of some doubt whether the authorities will allow him to go to Stockholm to collect his prize.

MASTERPIECE

Today, Neasden, a recluse-like figure held in low esteem by fellow Neasdenians, lives in a shabby, derelict outhouse just off the North Circular road.

Yesterday a group of correspondents representing the world's press made several attempts to speak to Mr Neasden.

Two reporters, including a Mr O'Booze, clambered over the 10 ft high barbed wire fence that surrounds the famous novelist's hideaway.

After breaking down the door of the house the bearded face of Neasden's greatest living writer appeared from an upstairs window.

Mr O'Booze then shouted: "Greetings, comrade. The world is waiting to pay its respects to overpowering genius."

By way of reply Mr Neasden threw some objects at Mr O'Booze and shouted some words which were drowned in the mighty roar of the North Circular road.

YES, THEY'RE THERE!

by Murray Mint

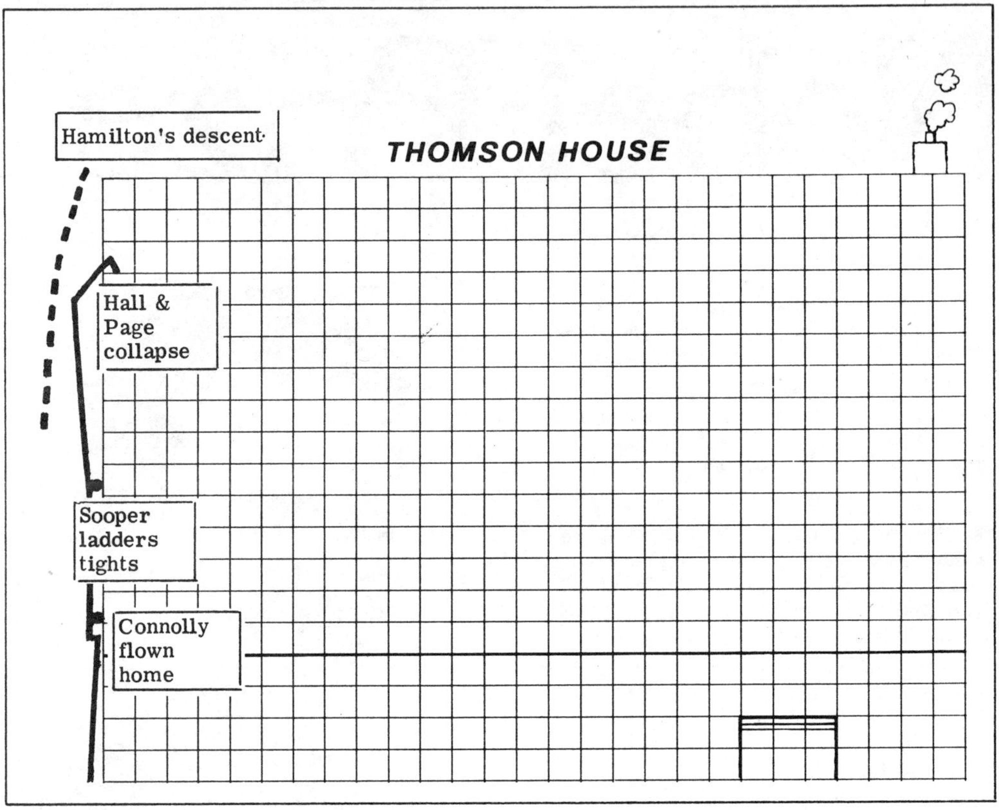

On top of the world! That was the message flashed to the world yesterday from the Gnome 1971 International Thomson House Expedition.

It was 11.31 Neasden Time, when tired but triumphant British climbers Ron Hall and Bruce Page at last planted the Thomson pennant on the summit of Thomson House, the highest building in Gray's Inn Road.

Ron Hall of Fame

Although Thomson House has been scaled more than 70 times over the years, this is the first time it has been climbed as a publicity stunt.

The Gnome expedition, sponsored by the Gnome press empire in collaboration with the BBC and Gannex Rubber Goods Inc., has captured the imagination of the world.

For months, the expedition up the infamous North Wall of Thomson House (only attempted before by two German window-cleaners in the winter of 1964), has been plagued by every imaginable mishap.

The troubles began last December, shortly after the 97-man team had established its Base Camp. No sooner had the camp, a small portable tent, been pitched on the Grays Inn Road pavement, than P C Ned Strangelove (or "The Odd Copper" as he is known) asked the expedition to "move along" as it was committing an offence under Section 2716 of the Public Buildings (Mountaineering Expeditions) Act of 1931.

Writer's Crampon

Next came the shock resignation from the expedition of Irish-born gastronaut and bon viveur Cyril Connolly, in protest against having to eat pate-de-foie gras from a tin. His body was flown home last week to a civic reception in his native Neasden, involving 250, 000 fans (*see* OAP's Waltz in Streets With Teenagers at Connolly Homecoming - Picture p 94).

Following the Connolly incident, the expedition ran into further trouble at the fourth floor, when progress was impeded by the body of Brigadier C D "Dennis" Hamilton hurtling through the air on his way to the pavement, in the course of his heroic one-man attempt on the Fifth-Floor-to-ground-level Executive Crash Course All Comers' Record. It is understood that Brig. Hamilton's record-breaking descent was inspired by the perusal of the latest *Times'* balance sheet, showing a marked downward tendency.

Fit of Peak

It was only two weeks ago, as the advance party neared the infamous "Chairman's Suite" on the 15th floor, that further disaster struck, when the only woman member of the team, Chelsea-born Jolly Sooper laddered her tights. As she was rushed across the road for emergency treatment in the back-seat of a new Leyland Marina (*see* The Car You've Waited For All Your Life by Motoring Correspondent Bamber Gasket - p 94), many male members of the team threw up their hands in protest, only to find themselves in the company of the now motionless Brigadier on the pavement below. (*see* Stop This Pavement Body Horror - What the Eye Thinks - p 94).

Private Eiger

It was shortly after this incident that the two surviving members of the expedition claim to have had a good sight of the mysterious Abominable Snowdon, a small furry creature which snaps at all who come near it.

However, the reliability of this report can only be considered in the light of the party's subsequent experience when negotiating the infamous "Director's Window."

This vertical wall, as smooth as glass (for indeed that is the substance of which it is made) proved as treacherous as ever. As Hall's lean, suntanned knees came into contact with the wall, there was a nasty crack and both men found themselves falling several inches into a deep carpet, where they lay semi-conscious for some seconds.

When they came to, they discovered a large cocktail cabinet in perfect condition. On investigation, they found several untouched bottles, still bearing original labels, such as Glen Thomson Genuine-Scotch-Style-Japanese-Malt-Drink - "The Whisky The Astronauts Like To Drink."

A massive search for the two mountaineers by cleaning lady Mrs Noreen de Vere Harmsworth, 67, resulted early this morning in the discovery of the two men lying under the overhanging mahogany writing desk in a "critical" condition. Snatching the miniature brandy flask strapped to her back, the two men rapidly regained unconsciousness.

Summit's Up

Meanwhile a storm of criticism has broken in rival newspapers. It is alleged that the Thomson House expedition has been a "complete fiasco" and that the BBC has wasted thousands of pounds on a useless project, which could have been put to better use, such as helping to spread Sir Kenneth Clark's "Civilisation" to the under-civilised world.

But last night, BBC spokesman Chris Brash lashed back at the critics. "They are an ignorant bunch of twits" he lashed. "The expedition has been a 100% success, from our point of view, if not from that of the mountaineers, many of whom have fallen to their deaths. We have learned a tremendous lesson from this expedition - that is to say that we must never do anything like it again."

Mr Brash is 73.

GLENDA SLAG

FOR THE FIRST TIME EVER IN PRINT...
SOCCER'S HOTTEST PROPERTY

Bert O'Relli tells ALL

The loves, the loneliness, the goals, the girls, the clothes brushes

(One of the items listed is the odd one out. Can you spot it? Take your time. Answer p. 94)

"Um. I don't know what's the matter with me. I'm just not getting them in like I used to. When I first started I got three a week on average. But this season I haven't had one."

That was Bert O'Relli - talking to me frankly, fearlessly and outspokenly at his £50,000 custom-built hideaway home on the outskirts of Neasden's North Circular Road yesterday.

Tragic

Last week Bert was in the news again when he failed to show up at a training session called by controversial and tight-lipped Neasden manager, Ron Knee, 59.

It was the fifth time this year that Bert has disobeyed orders from his club chief. Yet another black mark in the fast-growing book of bloomers by this irresistible playboy in tight shorts and woolly socks who has become a living legend in his lifetime.

Just what is it that threatens to destroy the most promising footballer since Rudolf Valentino ?

Heartbreak

"Er. Frankly I don't know," he frankly confessed to me with a flash of that famous O'Relli charm that few women can resist. "What have you got on tonight Glenda ?"

He takes off his clothes and gets into bed with the grace of a gazelle and the speed of a cheetah. I felt a glimpse of that compelling something that sets Neasden Bridge Stadium on fire every Saturday afternoon.

Sorrow

I asked him about Shiondaigh O'Telegraoith, the lovely 17-year-old daughter of Daly O'Telegraoith, the hideous 71-year-old Irish actor with whom O'Relli's name has been romantically linked.

"Never mind that darling," he said, skilfully evading the question as he would a line of Dollis Hill half backs. "I can take on anything after I've had a few drinks - even the Dollis Hill half backs."

Tragedy

Say what you like, this tortured and sensitive young man is walking on a tightrope between failure and success, laughter and tears, joy and sadness, eggs and bacon.

I asked him what the future had in store. How could he come to terms with the pressures of being the world's most highly-paid soccer idol. "Come over here, thingy. I haven't got all afternoon," he told me.

I left him as I had found him. Still in search of something - probably his trousers.

(A Glenda Slag Exclusive)

"LET'S STOP THE KNOCKING" — pleads Knee

by Our Man in the Press Box who has to lean over and ask a bloke on the terrace "Who scored?"

Controversial tight-lipped Neasden manager, Ron Knee, 59, last night lashed out at critics of his new "safety first" tactics.

Said an ashen-faced Knee: "We got the result didn't we ? So let's stop the knocking and get on with the game."

Defence

Criticism of manager Knee's strategy first sprung up following the now legendary Neasden v Dollis Hill North Circular Trophy 2nd Leg Qualifying round in which the Neasden squad packed the defending goal for the entire match.

While five players stood in the goal, another five crouched on their shoulders, thus forming an impenetrable wall against which the Dollis Hill strikers, already weakened by injury, were totally ineffective.

Midfield dynamo, Irish-born Bert O'Relli was given the strenuous job of marking the Dollis Hill forwards.

Shock

So well marked were they that four of them (including international Ken Mostyn-Owen, 41) have filed a High Court action claiming loss of earnings as a result of losing valuable TV commercial contracts due to facial disfiguration.

Last night a tired but triumphant Knee lashed back: "We got the goal didn't we ? And that's what counts to my mind."

LATE SCORE

North Circular Trophy 2nd Leg (Qualifying Round)

Dollis Hill 1 (O'Relli o.g.) — Neasden 0

Knee's team just one big yawn

says Dud Fivers, Soccer's Mr Football

The Greek squad to face Neasden in the second leg of the Inter-Suburbs European Nations Cup was named in Athens yesterday.

It reads: Xenophon, Egganchipolatas, Aristophanes, Menopaus, Owotalotigotides, Kikiminthebolox, Logarithm, Thucydides, Chrystalpallas, Underneathearchas Delicatessen.

FLOP

I see no point in listing Knee's so-called squad. There are about as many shocks in it as a run-down torch battery.

I don't have to write them down. I've written them so many times, I could do it in my sleep.

RUBBISH

Knee's eleven is as predictable as tomorrow's weather and twice as gloomy.

If you suffer from insommia try reading this:

1	R Norris	41
2	D Pevsner	39
3	L Watford	56
4	B Watford	42
5	T Longford	63
6	K McPong	42
7	L Essoldo	36
8	R Throat	46
9	P F Carter-Ruck	72
10	B O'Relli	19
11	S Dulwich	41
Sub:	P Marnham	49

"See what I mean Sergeant ! Pakistanis can't stand the smell of a bacon sandwich!"

"If what you say is correct, and that is John Wayne the country really is in a hell of a mess."

"These are fine, I'll take these."

STRAVINSKY

Before he died Stravinsky had been approached by David Frost and had agreed to give him an interview. Owing to the tragic death of the great composer, however, the interview never took place.

But now thanks to the miracle of modern technology it is possible by means of electronic computers to reconstruct the interview, exactly as it would have been had it taken place. Every single known fact about the two participants was fed into the giant G.N.O.M.I.E. (General Neo-Ontological Memory Intelligence Extractor) at Chipping Neasden and the interview, we are assured, is as close to the real thing as makes no difference.

The Interview that never took place

FROST: Hello. Good Evening and Welcome. And a very big hand for the world's greatest composer, the very wonderful Igor Stravinsky. *(Claps. Laughs).*

Igor, of all the many wonderful melodies that have flowed from your pen over your very long and wonderful lifetime, which is your favourite ?

STRAVINSKY: I like them all the same.

FROST: No but Igor, there must be one of all the many hundreds that you find yourself whistling in the bath more than others ?

STRAVINSKY: Quite wrong.

FROST: Seriously though, Igor, if you were cast away on a desert island which ONE of your gramophone records would you chose to take.

STRAVINSKY: I do not like the gramophone.

FROST: No, I know, but just supposing for the sake of argument .... Let me put it another way, supposing your life depended on your having to name your favourite melody that you had written, which would you name ?

STRAVINSKY: You must be kidding.

FROST: *(drawing gun):* No I'm not Igor. You have precisly two minutes to choose your one best tune.

STRAVINSKY: Now I've seen everything.

FROST: And while we're waiting let's listen to one of your best loved melodies, the very famous and very popular *Firebird Serenade* sung by our very own, very loveable Clodagh Rodgers.

STRAVINSKY: I love it. I love every single note of it.

(Frost giggles hysterically, claps wildly and shoots himself. Stravinsky administers last Rites of Spring. Closedown. Weather. Queen).

The Life of Dr. JONATHAN

being an account of the life and times of the celebrated
DR JONATHAN MILLER,

by his devoted companion and amanuensis

John Boswells

1

On the 17th September 1971, I came across the great doctor seated amid a circle of admirers in that tavern known as the "BBC Club" in Shepherds Bush. On my remarking that I had heartily enjoyed his latest dramatic rendering of *The Death of Danton,* never before performed on account of its extreme length and tedium, but which he had refurbished as it were a piece new-minted yesterday, he replied with his customary vigour:

JONATHAN: Sir, you are right. It is a brilliant piece, which I have rescued from oblivion solely by the operation of my own genius.

BOSWELLS: I congratulate you, sir, and would wish heartily to concur with your judgement. It is to be doubted whether there has ever been, or shall ever be again, such a triumph of the dramatic art.

JONATHAN: Sir, I must venture to contradict you. Even now I have in train a project beside which the *Danton* will seem but a candle to the rays of the sun. I refer to my proposal to adapt *Julius Caesar* for the stage.

BOSWELLS: Doctor, you amaze me. Pray enlighten me further on this project.

JONATHAN: I discovered one day, while leafing among some dusty volumes, this obscure piece, the work of some Jacobean hack whose name escapes me.

On my venturing to suggest that the author in question might be the celebrated William Shakespeare, self-styled "Swan of Avon," the Doctor hastened to brush my interjection aside.

JONATHAN: Sir, it matters not whose the piece was. Suffice it to say that it will soon be so transformed by my genius, that it will in future be known as no-one's but my own.

At this the company cheered and clapped, the great Doctor himself leading the applause. Motioning us at length to silence, he continued:

JONATHAN: I shall present this account of affairs in ancient Rome as if it were set in the Americas of the present day. The similarity of the central figure, Caesar, to the late President Kennedy cannot have escaped you.

BOSWELLS: No indeed, Doctor.

JONATHAN: But of course, the real

interest of the piece lies in the character of the ghost. Here to be sure we see that Shakespeare, like myself, was fascinated by the strange phenomenon of Victorian spiritualism, and I propose to rewrite the play in order to bring this out more fully.

BOSWELLS: Brilliant, Jonathan, brilliant. It is an inspired idea, and should arouse the public to scenes of unbridled enthusiasm.

JONATHAN: For once, Boswells, you are right. I am indeed a genius, and I will thank you for letting the world know that fact.

BOSWELLS: Sir, I endeavour to give satisfaction.

2

I journeyed today to Oxenford, to attend the opening night of the Doctor's new tragedy JULIUS CAESAR in three acts, adapted from the stage from the original by Wm. Shakespeare. I have seldom been so heartily rewarded by any theatrical piece. Afterwards in a nearby tavern, the Gloucester Arms, I discovered the great man seated amid a throng of admirers and fresh-faced scholars.

BOSWELLS: Doctor, you have excelled yourself with this piece. Truly your suggestion that the players should perform in body-stockings to convey the timelessness of the drama is a stroke of matchless genius.

DR JONATHAN: Sir, say no more. The world has seen nothing yet of my genius.

At this the crowd roared their approval, the Doctor himself leading the applause - but at length, motioning us to silence, he continued:

DR JONATHAN: Now gentlemen, I crave your pardon. I must return this night to the capital where I am to address a combined meeting of the Royal Society and the British Academy on the subject of Thinking Out the Future. It shall be my aim to show that the greatest works of science-fiction are those which deal not with the future but with the past. Indeed the greatest masterpiece in this genre is the *Recherche du Temps Perdu* of Marcel Proust.

At this brilliant paradox, the table fell on a roar. Amid the clamour and cries of bravo, it was observed that one young man was circulating copies of a lampoon, lately published in the capital, holding up the great Doctor to ridicule and vulgar satire. Upon espying this, the Doctor flew into a violent distemper. Waving his hands about like some oriental dervish, and his face empurpled with rage, he cried:

DR JONATHAN: Sir, the men responsible for these outrages are nothing but dogs, rats, toads and like vermin. There is but one fit place for such craven hacks - namely the hospital of Bedlam!

It was only when I heartily assured the Doctor that the great lamp of his genius remained undimmed by such trivial gibes, that his humour returned to its normal benevolent condition.

3

I discovered the great Doctor seated amid a throng of admirers at his usual table in the BBC Club in Shepherd's Bush. I ventured to congratulate him on his recent television essay concerning the city of New York.

JONATHAN: Sir, I am obliged to you for your perceptive felicitations. You are not alone in regarding this film as a work of the highest genius, portraying the city as a microcosm of the human condition. What I have tried to do in this piece is to convey a sense of the frenzied despair that co-exists with an immensely exciting emptiness reminiscent of the canvases of de Chirico.

As I reached for my quill to transcribe these pearls of the Doctor's wisdom, he continued:

JONATHAN: I am sure, Sir, that the novelty of these sentiments will be evident to you. No one has ever spoken with such perception on this subject before, unless it be J P Morgenblum's masterpiece *The City: Icon of Hell.*

BOSWELLS: Doctor, the range of your learning never ceases to astonish me.

JONATHAN: Sir, the finest sight the British visitor to New York ever sees is the BOAC plane waiting to return him to London!

At this, the company fell on a roar, one young acolyte becoming so convulsed at the profundity of the Doctor's sally that he fell into an apoplexy and was carried off to Bedlam.

4

It was on a December evening in 1971, that I next encountered the Doctor, at the house of his neigbour, the distinguished voluptuary and critick Prof. Geo. Melly.

JONATHAN (smiling): The British Broadcasting Corporation is to be congratulated on the sagacity of its latest enterprise, which should add greatly to the diversion and instruction of the nation.
MELLY: Burp!
BOSWELLS: Pray, sir, what is this enterprise of moment to which you refer so warmly ?
JONATHAN: Why, sir, to their intention to refurbish for modern ears the old "Brain's Trust." You will doubtless recall how in the darkest days of The Seven Years War, the torch of learning was weekly carried to millions by means of Mr Marconi's ingenious device.
BOSWELLS: Indeed, Doctor, I recall it as if it were but "All Our Yesterdays."
MELLY: Burp!
JONATHAN: But who, you will ask, in the decline of our own time, could hope to match the philosophical cunning of Professor Joad, the sound nautical bottom of Commander Campbell or the scientific erudition of Sir Julian Huxley?
BOSWELLS: Well, sir, I cannot rightly say.
JONATHAN: Sir, there is one man alive today whose genius not only embraces theirs, but shines above them all.
BOSWELLS: Pray, sir - this paragon of whom you speak. Could it be Lord Goodman ?
JONATHAN: Idiot! I will give you one more chance.
BOSWELLS: For the life of me, Doctor, I

am unable to answer. Pray tell me, who is this grand Panjandrum of all the Sciences to whom you refer ?
JONATHAN: (highly incensed): Why, you Scots dunderhead - MYSELF!

At this, the great Doctor seized hold of a cheese standing by, and hurled it across the table at my head. But as fortune would have it, it struck instead the now recumbent form of Professor Melly, who looking up, peered briefly about him in a bewildered manner, before sinking gratefully back into the arms of Oblivion.

5

I had enjoyed no converse with the Doctor for some weeks, when early in the month of February I received a summons to dine with him at his lodgings in Gloucester Crescent. As I entered the room, I perceived the Doctor seated amid a large and convivial company, which included Mr Geo. Melly, the celebrated bon viveur and critic, Mr Nicholas Tomalin, scribbler of those days and Prof. Dworkin, a most learned jurisprudent lately shipped from the plantations and now resident at Oxenford.

Boswells: Intelligence has reached me, Doctor, that you are engaged to produce the Taming of the Shrew for the forthcoming Dramatic Festival at Chichester. This will surely mark the zenith of the theatrical season.

Dr Jonathan: Sir, you are right. I have no doubt that my interpretation of this piece will command universal approbation and provide the centrepiece for all cultivated conversation.

Melly: I think the pot is with you, Doctor. Be so good as to circulate it.

Boswells: How will you render this most diverting of the Bard's comedies ?

Dr Jonathan (incredulously): Comedies, sir ? This piece is no comedy, but the most pathetic and tenebrous of all Shakespeare's tragedies.

Boswells: Sir, this surely surpasses even your gift for paradox ?

Dr Jonathan: Why, sir, it is only dunderheads and poltroons who would take this play to be a comedy ...

Melly: ... Groove it, man!

Dr Jonathan: ... In the Taming of the Shrew we perceive a theme most relevant to our own times - to wit, the curbing and subjugation of the proud spirit of womanhood by the blind and insensitive tyranny of the male chauvinist ...

Dworkin (interrupting): ... I would agree that the Women's Liberation Movement is one of the most extraordinary and fascinating developments in the present stage of cultural evolution. I see it very much in the context of a kind of cross-fertilisation between Rousseau-ite libertarianism, Mid-Western populist neo-Bryanism of the type which produced the Prohibition movement and Polynesian ...

Melly: Burp, burp.

Dr Jonathan: Sir, you have imposed on our polite restraints for too long with this Yankee gibberish. Pray be silent, and give room to someone of more summary phrase and concise philosphy.

Boswells: But, sir, you are not one to talk.

Dr Jonathan (smiling): Sir, I do little else!

At this sally, surely one of the most apposite ever delivered even by the great Doctor himself, the company fell on a roar, and Mr Tomalin on his face (he having been lulled into a slumber by the Professor's harangue).

6

I discovered the doctor at his lodgings in Gloucester Crescent, seated by candlelight, Dr Franklin's electrical apparatus having been temporarily incommoded by the dereliction of certain discontented mechanics. He was surrounded, as ever, by an admiring *levée*, which included Prof. Dworkin, the learned jurisprudent from the plantations. Mr Geo Melly, the critick, Mr Alan Bennett, a provincial dramatist of the sentimental school, and Mistress Tweedie, an emancipated woman of the new mode.

BOSWELLS: It cannot have escaped your notice, Doctor, that a certain sheet lately circulated among the gin shops of Grub Street, namely the *Cosmopolitan* (for it is so called), has named you as a most desir-

TERRIBLE OLD JOKE

(AS TOLD TO SPIKE MILLIGAN)

MAN IN RESTAURANT: "Waiter! There's a fly in my soup!"
WAITER; "Never mind, Sir. The spider on the bread roll will get him."

able paramour for Mistress Cooper, the groaning bawd.
DOCTOR: Sir, this is a vile enterprise of which I will have no part. The woman is nothing but a notorious slut and fishwife. Be so good as to furnish me with several copies, that I may peruse them at my leisure.
DWORKIN: (having been unusually silent for several minutes)I'd like to come in here, if I may, with a comment on the strange predicament which has resulted from the failure in the electrical power supply. We find ourselves in a kind of pre-McLuhanesque environment, totally deprived of audio-tactile sensory stimuli....
TWEEDIE: Woops!
MELLY: No offence, sir or madam.
DR.JONATHAN: Pray spare us any further of your laborious disquisitions, Professor, and allow me to proceed with my own. This temporary cessation in the supply of electrical current is indeed discommoding, but I thank you to reflect on the benign dispensation of Providence whereby the nation was not deprived of my recent discourse, through the medium of Mr. Marconi's device, concerning the works of Geo. Stubbs, the painter of horses.
BOSWELLS: Indeed, sir, it was a contribution to public instruction and pleasure surpassing anything I can recall. Your astonishing versatility in all fields of learning and Science is surely an eighth Wonder of the Age.
DR.JONATHAN: I am obliged to you, Sir, for your just discernment and for the veracity of your observation. And now, I must beg leave of you all. The post-chaise is at the door which is shortly to convey me to Heathrow.
BOSWELLS: Sir, for what purpose do you wish to travel to that desolate place?
DR.JONATHAN: Dunderhead! Are you not aware, sir, that this heath in Middlesex has lately become the chief station for the balloonist M. Montgolfier's admirable aerial conveyances?
DWORKIN: The balloon is certainly a most remarkable development in the evolution of transportation techniques....

DR.JONATHAN(smiling): Indeed, sir, it is, for it is the only device known to man which is more filled with hot air than yourself. But to resume my narrative - the purpose of my voyage is that I am engaged to re-enact the Tragedy of Richard II before the colonial inhabitants of Los Angeles.
BOSWELLS: Would not such a piece seem excessively antique to the denizens of a region so famed for their devotion to contemporaneity?
DR.JONATHAN: You are right, sir, and to this end I have refurbished the piece in the style of the 1930's. My leading player, Mr. Richard Chamberlain, will interpret Richard II in the person of the ill-fated Duke of Windsor. The many parallels between these two royal histories are too evident to enlarge upon.

As the Doctor rose to take his leave of us, gesticulating wildly as was his wont, his elbow overturned the candelabrum, plunging the company into a Stygian blackness.
TWEEDIE: Woops! Male chauvinist pig!

Upon the Doctor striking his tinderbox, a scene was revealed so singular that it was beyond my sense of decorum and discretion to describe it.

7

It being a fine spring day, the Doctor bestowed on me the signal privilege of allowing me to accompany him on a perambulation of Sir Solomon Zuckermann's Zoological Gardens in Regent's Park.

As we paused in reverence before my Lord Snowdon's ingenious device for the trapping of birds, the envy of any rustic fowler, the great Doctor seemed in high spirits. The clemency of the season and the lavish encomia which had been showered by the criticks on his latest dramatic offering, had combined to rouse him utterly from his customary melancholy.
DR.JONATHAN (smiling): Sir, there are more ideas fluttering in my head than there are birds in this cage.
BOSWELLS: To be sure, Doctor. I perceive you are described by Mr. Lewsen in the *Times* newspaper as our nearest approximation in these latter days to the giants of the Renaissance. Indubitably one must return to such mighty men of old as Michael Angelo, Sir Philip Sidney or the great Leonardo himself to find any counterpart.
DR.JONATHAN: Sir, you speak no more than the truth. Why, I have now in hand no less than seventeen dramatic productions, any one of which I venture to assert would be sufficient to establish me as the rightful successor to Sir Tyrone Guthrie. Furthermore, my reputation as a philosopher of medicine is daily growing, and only this week have I concluded a monograph on the great Sir Charles Sherrington
BOSWELLS: Who?
DR.JONATHAN: Dunderhead! Are you such a simpleton that you are not familiar with the name of the 'Faraday of Phrenology'?

You will be telling me next you have never heard of Schlumpft.
BOSWELLS: I have never heard of Schlumpft.
DR.JONATHAN: But this is not all. For many years I have had in train an enterprise so monumental, so exacting, and so far-reaching in its philosophical erudition that our civilisation has known nothing like it since the Tractatus Monolithico-Absurdicus of Von Büttlegger. I refer to my 50-volume treatise, now in preparation, on the subject of mesmerism in the 19th century, in which I shall seek to establish beyond doubt the connection between Victorian mesmerists, the Benthamite Neo-Hegelians, the Renaissance Platonists, St Thomas Aquinas, the paintings of Claes Oldenburg, the rise of Judaeo-Christian monotheism, the collapse of the Weimar Republic, and the invention of Dr.Sweeting's patent Knee Absorber in 1872.
BOSWELLS: Sir, what is mesmerism, sir?

At this the Doctor became even more animated than before, and with wild gesticulations, contortions of the facial muscles and twitchings, continued to hold forth with astonishing eloquence for upwards of several hours, at which singular demonstration, I eventually passed into a deep slumber. Upon waking, I recognised that I had been the subject of a practical exhibition of the art of mesmerism, such as no words could justly convey.

(To be continued)

DWORKIN: Why aren't I in this week?

Radio3

VHF; and 464m (647kHz), 194m (1546kHz) or 188m (1594kHz)

Benjamino Luckhurst sings in NEASDEN HO! the afternoon opera at 10.15

11.0

Test Match Special

Hans Killer discusses the influence of Schönberg on the bowling of Chandrasekar Ravi-Shankar (4-31).

11.15

Afternoon Sequence

A sequence of music composed in the key of B-Flat Minor by composers whose names begin with F while under the influence of drugs.

11.30

The Young Mendlessohn

The fourth in a series.
Beethoven: Symphony No 9 in D Minor.
Dallapicolla: Two pieces.
Tippett: Fantasia on a Theme by Myself.+
Myself: Requiem for Solo Kazoo: In Memoriam Lord Reith.
Armstrong: S O L Blues.
Neasden String Quartet with Cecil Aronowitz (kazoo).

+ First Broadcast Perf.

11.37

In the interval Hans Killer talks to John Arlott about the lunchtime influence of *Mouton Cadet* (1849) on speech coherency during the afternoon.

In the interval of the talk, Hans Killer will discuss the influence of Schönberg on the kazoo players of the Vienna Riding School.

12.15

The Young Idea

Leo Bleck talks about the early influence of Schönberg on the early career of the little known Lithuanian composer Pyotr Idea (1890-1924) whose only work, the Symphony No 14, can be heard at this year's Promenade Concerts on August 29th.

1.04

News and Weather

News: Suite - The Kentuckian (1941).
Weather: Overture Ohio (1952).
Eugene Ormandy conducts the Hollywood Bowl Philharmonic Symphony Orchestra.

1.50

Lunchtime Scoreboard

2.00

Masterworks

A series in which the great undisputed masterpieces of music are played for the first time (introduced by Leo Bleck). *Boris Mozart:* Trumpet Concerto in C. *Bleck:* Song Cycle "Das Picled-herring." *Leslie Haydn:* Theme and variations for Harp and flute (Op 3,426).

In the interval Cecil Aronowitz talks to Leo Bleck about the particular problems of playing the kazoo after a lifetime spent playing the viola.

5.29

Midday Concert

Stockhausen: Infra Dig - Three.
Bax: To the Wall (1940).
Mondrian: Overture " The Pickwick Papers."
Neasden Symphony Orchestra (leader: Monty Balmoral. Conductor: Sviatoslav Perrins.

6.15

Jazz in Britain

The Indian composer Dongivamealldat Jazz (1943-) recently gave a series of concerts at the Three Queers Festival, Neasden - on-Stour, in which he lectured and demonstrated the art of playing the dringi, a gong-like percussion instrument played with the teeth.

In the interval, Hans Killer discusses the difficulty of dredging up more and more tenth rate old musical junk to fill up his schedules with.

ELIZABETH AND LONGFORD

By LADY MAGNESIA FREELOVE

(As Told to John Wells)

One of the most extraordinary figures to erupt onto the stage of the second Elizabethan Age was Frank Orgier Pakenham, 94th Earl of Longford. Statesman, banker, socialist, prison visitor, author, publisher Earl - he seemed a glittering exemplar of the explosion of talent and versatility that typified that larger-than-life era.

He first steps onto our stage in the spring of 1971. A tall, gangling, balding figure, with wisps of hair surrounding his shining pate, and a high aristocratic voice, he was by any account, an unlikely candidate for the favours of the ageing Queen.

Yet it remains a fact that on St George's Day in that year, the people of London were awakened to hear the astonishing news that Queen Elizabeth had bestowed upon the Earl the highest honour in her gift, namely a Knighthood of the Garter.

Never before in history had this honour been granted to anyone other than former Prime Ministers, military heroes who had saved the nation and foreign monarchs.

Bonham Garter

When the news filtered out from Windsor that Her Majesty had elevated Lord Longford in this fashion the Court buzzed for days with speculation.

In that rip-roaring, swashbuckling renaissance that was the Britain of the 1970s, Longford outshone the rest in his pursuit of all that was new and extraordinary.

Scarcely a pornographic film could have its premiere, without his well-publicised presence in the audience. His loping, mackintoshed figure was familiar to the denizens of Soho's most disreputable resorts. His friendships with some of the most notorious rakes and criminals of the time were the small-change of every scribbler and satirist in London. Only weeks before the news of his honour, it was announced that he had befriended Mistress Hindley, the most infamous witch and child-slayer of her day, and rumour had it that he had even introduced into her place of confinement the rites of the Papish mass. Some months before that, his name had been widely associated with the treasons and stratagems of the so-called "Aitken Plot," when the editor of the *Sunday Telegraph* had been stretched upon the rack for several days to the vast amusement of the populace.

This was the man, whose name could scarce be uttered aloud in polite society without provoking gales of unseemly mirth, whom the Queen had chosen out from all her subjects to be installed in the Chapel of St George at Windsor as "her own most puissant and gentil chevalier, nobly-fronted jouster sans pareil, most parfit quaestor and sillie old twytte."

It was a sign of the Queen's growing isolation from reality that she should have dared to incur the wrath and ridicule of the nation by so blatantly eccentric an appointment.

Why did she do it ? Even today, we are not really any nearer to a satisfactory answer than were Elizabeth's own astonished subjects at the time.

Perhaps it is not altogether fanciful to suggest that the Earl's flamboyant behaviour and colourful flouting of convention may have recalled to her mind another figure from the long-dead past - the ageing Queen's first love, Prince Philip II of Greece.

Whatever the explanation, there is no doubt that from the moment of his elevation, Longford's doom was sealed. He was sent shortly afterwards to put down the rebellion in Ulster, with the title of Viceroy. On his return from a complete military fiasco, he attempted to raise the standard of revolt by running amok in the City of London. He was joined, however, only by a handful of malcontents, and the rebellion ended ignominiously with his execution on Tower Hill.

"Goes against the grain, eh?"

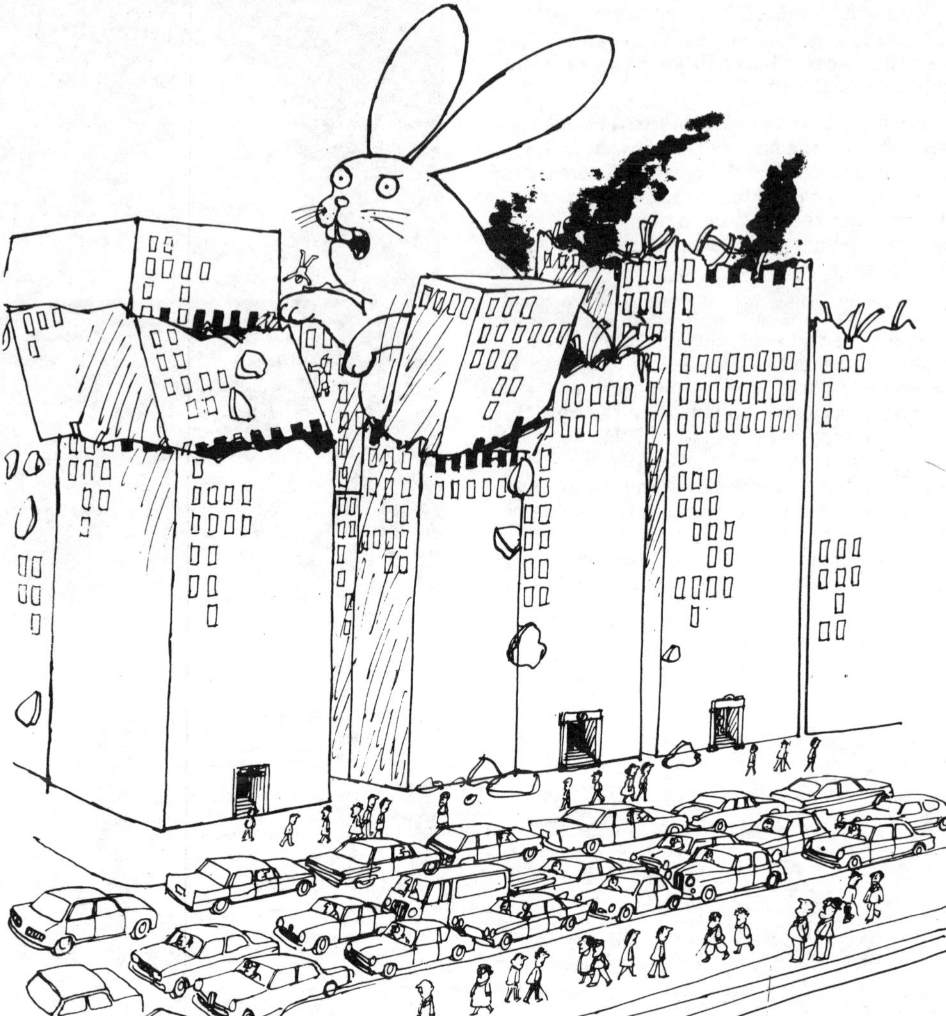

"I suppose if it was a gorilla, people would take it seriously."

THE TERRY COLEMAN INTERVIEW

"Come in and make yourself at home," he says. "Here, let me take your coat."

The Nonconformist of Neasden

HE LOOKS no older than his 46 years. You notice at first his face. It is at once both hestitant and expectant. His hand outstretched to shake one's own carries a message both of welcome and yet of privacy intruded upon. "Come in", he says. "Can I take your coat?" He moves across the room quickly and silently, as if he knows the terrain as well as a Grindelwald guide knows every foothold on the north face of the Eiger. It is a medium-sized room, at first sight much like thousands of others in this part of London. But then one's eye lights on the pile of telephone directories neatly stacked by the telephone; the bowl of fruit on the sideboard (one apple, two bananas). A television set stands unobtrusively in a corner, on its top an open copy of the *Radio Times*, with details of the *"Black and White Minstrel Show"* casually circled in blue biro.

"Would you like some tea? I'm just making some." His enquiry breaks into the silence like a polished pebble thrown precisely into the centre of a lily pond, sending vibrant ripples of expectancy through the room. "That would be nice," I reply, picking my words carefully, as a duellist may hesitate between the foil and the rapier. Without another word, he vanishes almost cat-like into the kitchen.

I wait, hearing distinctly the tick of the clock. From the kitchen comes the familiar rattle of cups and saucers being laid out on a tray. I feel somehow trapped by the vectors of the situation, for all the world like a stranger in someone else's house, waiting for him to bring in a cup of tea. "Won't be a minute", he shouts from next door. Then, suddenly, almost shockingly, he is back. "Well, I expect you'd like to get to work", he says, with a smile. "It's in the cupboard under the stairs." The remark bursts in on my consciousness like a ray of sunlight piercing angry storm clouds. "The meter, I mean," he continues. I pause, momentarily thrown by the elusiveness of his thought-processes. "Why don't you people wear a uniform any more?" In a flash, I see his meaning, for indeed in my role as interrogator I am not so far-removed from the Gestapo Colonel in the Avenue Foch, staring into the eyes of his victim as the blinding white light burned down from behind my head.

"Come along, I'll show you," he says, with an air of frustration, almost of impatience. What is he going to show me, I wonder? We walk together into the hall, where he bends down and unlocks a small cupboard, with all the assurance of a master safebreaker cocking his ear to the fall of the tumblers in the combination lock. Then he is back on his feet, an almost triumphant smile playing about his mouth. "There you are, it's all yours", he says. I peer into the semi-darkness, where I find myself looking at a small black box, its front covered by a series of dials. From where I kneel, I can just discern a slowly rotating disc, delicately rimmed with scarlet paint. Almost at once, he is showing me to the door, and I am in the street again. The rain is beginning to fall.

HOW DO THESE AT THE TOP?

Make no mistake. The stress and strain of modern living holds most of us back from fulfilling our ambitions. -

From the moment we get up in the morning we are irritable and ex-exhausted. Even after 10 or 11 hours sleep.

Some of you might say: I am as fit as a fiddle. That's what YOU think.

But leading pysioneurasthenists - ie scientsts who study the health of the Human Body - all agree on one thing.

That when you're feeling 100% fit, that's the danger signal that means you could be heading for a serious illness.

And that's where GNOMO-STRATH - the miracle Elixir - comes in.

GNOMO-STRATH is an entirely natural product prepared in up-to-date laboratories in the heart of the Swiss Alps.

It is made to a secret formula discovered by the world-famous Swiss bio-chemist Karl S. Dirtibugger (1837-1899) from 176 different wild herbs gathered in their natural surroundings all over the world.

Read what these world-famous men and women have said about GNOMO-STRATH:

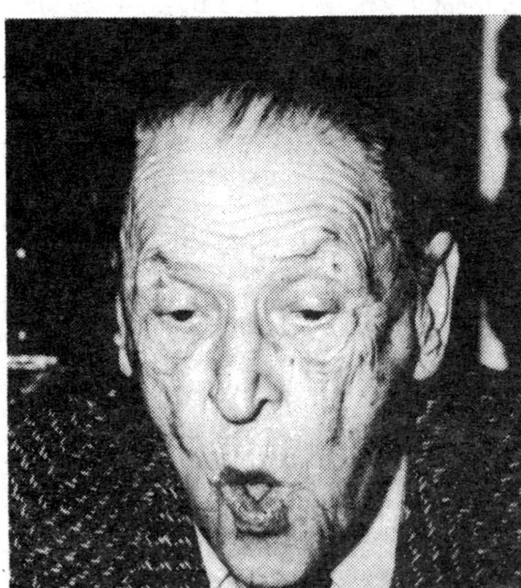

THE LATE SOMERSET MAUGHAM, world-famous story-teller, known to millions of readers all over the world: "Since taking GNOMO-STRATH I have been feeling a new man."

JOE GRUMMETT, world-famous international jockey: "Since drinking GNOMO-STRATH each morning, I have ridden more winners than ever before. So take a tip. Put your money on GNOMO-STRATH. At £5 a bottle it's the shortest price in the race. Please send cheque c/o Ludwig Wittgenstein, Turf Accountant, Market Neasden, Cambs."

PEOPLE STAY

BERT O'RELLI, world famous Neasden footballer: "Since ashen-faced Ron Knee, 59, put me on GNOMO-STRATH, my performance has increased 100%. Thanks to GNOMO-STRATH I am getting a lot of goals, not to mention a lot of gals. Get it ? Tee hee hee."

LORD CLARK OF CIVILISATION. World-famous TV personality and art historian: "What could be more agreeable than this hand-tooled bottle of herbal cordial culled from some of the rarest and most exquisite of Mother Nature's wild flora. How every spoonful breathes an air of the Swiss genius that gave the world the Alpenhorn, the cuckoo clock and the boomerang!" *(Adjusts exquisitely tailored swimming trunks. Takes running jump into Lake Geneva and sinks agreeably to the bottom.* AS SEEN ON TV).

YE OLDE MENUHIN (world famous herbal violinist and mystic): "Franz Schubert was a delightfully warm and gay human being. Some of the world's most beautiful melodies flowed from his pen in a sparkling stream of song. If only GNOMO-STRATH had been available to the curly-haired Franz, I am sure he would still be alive today!"

Nature's own passport to health, happiness and success

Grocer seen as Pompidou threat

From RICHARD BREEZE, "Herald" Correspondent

Sydney Morning Herald

CRUMPET

Sir, — Your correspondent "Muffin the Mule" is quite right to decry the absence of fresh crumpet in Guildford over the weekends, but if he was as old as I am, then he would appreciate that the genuine article is not available in any case.

Today's version is at the best, anaemic-looking and flat and doesn't warrant a second nibble. — Yours, etc.

S. G. COOK.

Park Farm,
Alfold.

Surrey Advertiser

Shrine defacers are named

Jerusalem, Feb 20.—A company specializing in the restoration of old synagogues was blamed publicly today for defacing Judaism's holiest shrine, the Wailing Wall.

A special committee appointed by Mrs Golda Meir, the Prime Minister, to investigate why four small hotels were hacked into the wall placed the responsibility on the staff of the Corporation for the Development and Restoration of the Jewish Quarter of the Old City.

The Times

MILK RACE

several places behind him.

It's a strong strategic base for next week's operation, but unfortunately Bayton, who would have been Edwards's natural deputy, is still suffering from his fall. He finished at New Brighton with the bunch, but his back still pains, and he felt every bum in the road.

It was Havelka, a Czech of whom we know very little, who opened

THE OBSERVER.

6.55 Stars on Sunday

NINA
ROGER WHITTAKER
GILLIAN HUMPHRIES
LOS PICAFLORES
THE BEVERLEY SISTERS
THE ARCHBISHOP OF CANTERBURY

TV Times